John Grant has been ⣿⣿⣿⣿⣿⣿ editor for the last six ye⣿⣿⣿⣿⣿ He lives in the West C⣿⣿⣿⣿⣿ graphic designer, and da⣿⣿⣿⣿⣿ *tory of Possibilities* and *The Book of Time* (both with Colin Wilson) and an anthology of Science Fiction stories, *Aries 1*. He is the author of *A Directory of Discarded Ideas* and *A Book of Numbers*. His serious study *Dreamers*, his hilarious spoof of pseudo-science *Sex Secrets of Ancient Atlantis*, and his novel *The Truth About the Flaming Ghoulies* are also published by Grafton Books. He is an experienced lecturer and broadcaster.

By the same author

Non fiction
Dreamers: A Geography of Dreamland
A Book of Numbers
A Directory of Discarded Ideas
The Directory of Possibilities (edited, with Colin Wilson)
A Book of Time (edited, with Colin Wilson)

Fiction
Sex Secrets of Ancient Atlantis
The Truth About the Flaming Ghoulies
Aries 1 (edited)

JOHN GRANT

The Depths of Cricket

A Random 22-Yard Stroll

GRAFTON BOOKS

A Division of the Collins Publishing Group

LONDON GLASGOW
TORONTO SYDNEY AUCKLAND

Grafton Books
A Division of the Collins Publishing Group
8 Grafton Street, London W1X 3LA

A Grafton Paperback Original 1986

ISBN 0-586-06504-0

Printed and bound in Great Britain by
Cox & Wyman Ltd, Reading

Set in Times

With all my love to

CATHERINE

in the hope that this book will show her
what she's missing – and why.

If the French noblesse had been capable of playing cricket with their peasants their châteaux would never have been burnt.

– G. M. Trevelyan

He preferred the lady to cricket – though he was an accomplished bat and, like his father, fielded boldly at cover-point; and she found him more comforting than cards – though she played very good bridge indeed.

– Eric Linlelater, *Juan in America*

CONTENTS

On Sunday 22nd April daddy started nets in cricit. He nedeed: 5 cups and a bottle of lemnade and a towle and a bag to carre them in.

Back at home me and my mum had fun.

– from the journal of Jane Barnett

INTRODUCTION

Harold Pinter is probably furious about the fact that he is on record as remarking: 'I tend to believe that cricket is the greatest thing that God ever created on Earth.' On any intellectual level the statement is of course nonsense . . . but I wonder.

There are many respects in which Man differs from the animals – more or less. For example, you can describe Man as the tool-using animal – but in so doing you'd be ignoring the fact that a fair number of animals use tools, not just the assumedly intelligent ones, such as chimps, but also some species of birds and fish. Again, you could say that Man is the animal which laughs – but then so do many pets, or so it appears, and certainly so do dolphins. Whatever peculiarly human trait you choose, you can find an example of its imitation in the animal world. Except, possibly, one: the powerful desire to take part in games whose rules are simultaneously artificial and yet rigidly adhered to. Of all such games, a few stand out as fitting the definition particularly aptly: chess, for example, or bridge, or Go. Among the sports in this category, which involve both cerebral and physical activity, there seems in my admittedly bigoted view to be only the one contender: cricket.

To the outsider, cricket's rules are of course a nonsense: as someone once remarked, the game is, in essence, a matter of people throwing hard balls at soft ones. To someone involved in cricket, on the other hand – whether as a participant or merely as a spectator – the game is more important than trivia such as income or where the next meal's coming from. While generally a player or a supporter will back one particular team, that same person will receive a greater emotional reward from seeing the opposition win a good game than from seeing the 'home' side win a bad one. The teams will fight as hard as possible during the match, giving no quarter, but afterwards will exchange drinks and stories in the most friendly fashion. I was once at a Somerset *vs*. Yorkshire match at Taunton when an exceedingly drunk Yorkshire supporter climbed up onto his seat and told everyone, in astonishingly explicit detail, quite how curious were the sexual predilections of the Somerset team and its followers. The reaction was general laughter and applause. If he'd done the same sort of thing at a football match he'd have been dead.

So the attraction – the sheer fascination – of cricket has little to do with mere partisanship. Of course, one wants one's 'own' side to win – but that's not the important thing: witness the fact that, around the boundary of any village cricket match, you are certain to find some spectators who do not even know the names or loyalties of the two competing sides. They are interested in the *game*.

This interest seems to be a fundamental part of the human make-up: we become fascinated by things which may not in themselves be terribly important. Let me cite a couple of examples. (1) There is in Britain a successful television programme called 'The Great Egg Race'. Each week teams of contestants are required to perform tasks using eggs which could almost certainly be more easily performed using other components in place of the eggs. The game is manifestly pointless . . . and yet, and yet, *is* it? Certainly the programme is utterly fascinating. Moreover, the ingenuity required to launch a balloon using half a dozen eggs, say, can well be applied more generally to rather more useful problems. In the apocryphal tale, Newton was able to explain not just why apples fell to Earth but how the entire Universe worked (well, as good as dammit); equally, some of the principles established by participants in 'The Great Egg Race' may well, in different manifestations, prove to be highly important. (2) The day before yesterday, I spent a happy hour and a half with two small children seeing if there was any way, between the three of us, that we could set up a system whereby a partially deflated ball would travel from the back of a child's bicycle down an old plank, over a tricycle, down the side of a rotting cardboard box and into a semi-demolished plastic baby-bath. A silly task – but the challenge was irresistible. Instantly, I noticed, and without discussion certain rules were created: for example, it was forbidden to give the ball any initial impetus; it had to roll of its own free will. None of us questioned the value of the desired end-product of the exercise. We had created a game, and we were fascinated by it. We were exhibiting behaviour typical of human beings.

Of course, not all games concern trivia. Some people find it fun to play war-games – on occasion using real weapons and killing real people. The vast majority of the participants in such games are given no choice about whether or not they want to play.

Moving to less obscene games, we come to cricket. A good game of cricket, contested between teams whose players are of roughly equal ability, is as intricate as any war. There are minor risks of injuries to the participants – very occasionally, these may even be fatal – but the players are there out of choice. Deliberate attempts to increase the risks, as when fast bowlers stupidly send down bouncers at tail-enders, are generally discouraged, often even by the bowlers' own team-mates. As with

chess, the point of the 'war' is not to kill or maim –
indeed, the contest is, as I have implied, in many ways
not a physical one at all, but a mental one. Of course,
physical skills enter into it, but only insofar as a physically
far superior team will usually hammer an inferior one
assuming that the contestants are of equal mental skills.
However, the 'weaker' team may often defeat the
'stronger' if its various members – especially its captain –
use strategy and cunning as their allies. For example, in
the 1983 World Cup Final the Indians, led by Kapil Dev,
comfortably defeated the powerful West Indies because
the latter, one assumes, felt so assured of victory thanks
to the many brilliant cricketers in their side that they
didn't bother to think about the tactical aspects. The
Indians repeated the feat in a lesser championship in
1985. Conversely, the West Indians drubbed England in
the 1984 Test Series – by five matches to one, and
generally by a colossal margin – primarily because
England, while manifestly the weaker team, failed to
follow the Indians' cerebral example. Similarly, in 1984
when a contest was mounted to find the 'World's Greatest
All-Rounder' among Malcolm Marshall, Richard Hadlee,
Kapil Dev, Ian Botham and Clive Rice, Rice emerged as
victor purely because he had the wit to think about the
rules of the contest beforehand and to work out how best
to exploit them: in a sense, in so doing, he proved that he
was the 'World's Greatest All-Rounder'! (Imran Khan,
who might well lay claim to the title, was unfortunately
involved in the contest only from the television commentary box.)

Because the mental aspect of cricket is so important,
games can prove fascinating at all levels of the sport: a
bunch of schoolkids or even two teams of chartered
accountants can produce a game which is every bit as
exciting as any played at international level – and very

often much more exciting. Two well matched teams with their minds concentrated on winning will inevitably produce a good game, whatever their absolute merits . . . unless, of course, the pitch is appalling, the umpires deliberately or unconsciously bent, the visiting team subtly scuttled by Mrs Jones' delicious but super-dense Dundee cake, and so on, and so on. In other words, there are certain little variables to be found in the lower classes of cricket which do not enter the first-class game.

Leaving that aside for the moment, though, it's worth spending a little time speculating about the reasons *why* games like cricket and chess are so fascinating. *Why* is it that the human mind should become so intensely involved in what are, after all, irrelevances? Can the phenomenon tell us something important about the human animal?

I think possibly it can. Consider the humble fruit-machine. Everybody knows that – unless you possess paranormal powers of some sort! – if you play fruit-machines over any period of time you are going to lose money. However, the things are fantastically popular: you can hardly go into a café or pub without seeing one or several of the machines, and generally speaking they are well used. Some people will spend hours on end, day after day, plugging coins into them and watching the reels spin. While casual users may have their sights set on short-term pecuniary gain ('I won't notice if I lose 50p but I will notice if I gain £3'), regular players must know, from both theory and practice, that they lose money. That they are happy to do so can only mean that they are deliberately or unconsciously reckoning that they are spending money in order to play the game – a point realized by the manufacturers of coin-slot videogame machines, expensive games software for your home computer, and so on. The fruit-machine game is a very simple one, and most modern machines require no skill at all on the part of the player, but clearly it fascinates the human mind.

I think it probably does so because our minds *require* stimulation – in some cases virtually constant, in others merely occasional. This may sound trite at first, but I'm not merely making a woolly point or penning platitudes (I hope). I think that the need for mental stimulation is every bit as profound and fundamental as the mind's *requirement* for rest and relaxation. Many years ago I knew someone who had the misfortune to work at the Ford car factory at Dagenham, which was then especially strike-prone. When I asked him why, he replied that it was because the staff facilities were 'not good'; because, if you went to the lavatory, within a few minutes the foreman would be hammering on the door telling you to get a move on; and so forth. I think he was right in part – but I think there was more to it than that. Workers will strike, even if they are already being paid over the odds, if their jobs are repetitive, monotonous and mind-numbing, and especially so if – according to my friend's description – there are no opportunities for mental stimulation even during the rest periods. The strike gives the workers something to think about, something to become involved in, some relief from the monotony, something to be a part of: in a way, you could describe it as a team game.

Ford have presumably realized this, because Dagenham rarely features in the newspapers these days. Volvo realized it years ago, and so introduced a system of manufacture whereby each worker had a job which was in itself interesting and satisfying, and he was also made to feel an important part of the company, of the team. Japanese car manufacturers, who insist that senior executives dine with the workforce, use this and other methods to ensure that each worker feels a part of the team – that each is helping towards the common goal of 'winning the game'.

From my own personal experience, the equivalence of the two requirements for rest and stimulation is a very real one. If I spend all my day working at something extremely interesting and mentally demanding, in the evening I'll probably want just to sit with my mouth open watching some garbage on the television. If I've been doing something boring all day I'm much more likely to want to spend my evening, even though I'm just as physically tired, reading a book – or, for that matter, playing cricket. Both relaxation and stimulation can be used in very similar ways to effect cures: if I find I'm both mentally and physically run down after a long period of concentrated work, I can either spend a day in bed resting or I can go out and spend the day doing something new which sparks my interest. I can combine the two, of course, by taking with me to bed a challenging book on a subject about which I know nothing, or by spending the day watching or playing a cricket match (when I play cricket, I get plenty of time for physical relaxation), or in various other ways.

If we can accept, then, the absolute necessity that the mind receive its daily dose of stimulation, we must next ask what it is in various games which gives them the necessary 'fascination-power'. This is difficult, because the games differ from person to person. I find cricket engrossing, but my daughter would, if the truth be told, far rather have a no-holds-barred game of Snap (she'll learn, she'll learn). My wife would rather do almost anything other than watch a game of cricket: while the games I am interested in are almost exclusively competitive, from cricket to crosswords (solver *vs* compiler), she is interested in noncompetitive games, such as painting. (I am not belittling painting by calling it a game: I am maintaining that games are of fundamental importance.)

What is it, then, which all games – competitive and noncompetitive – have in common that gives them the power to ensnare the human mind? The answer is complex, but one element must be the degree of comprehension of the game by the spectator or participant. For example, I find middle- and long-distance running competitions thrilling because I know enough about the underlying techniques to appreciate quite fully what is going on, but the 100m dash leaves me stone cold. Other people, who understand the 100m dash, find it very exciting but feel that the long-distance events are just that – long.

Added to the understanding of the rules and the techniques, however, has to be the fact that they must be sufficiently complicated. There must be some degree of difficulty with them. Recently my daughter, who has rather grown out of Snakes and Ladders because it's just too easy, came home with a game which was in fact identical with Snakes and Ladders but *looked* as if it were different: I should think she'll have grown out of it within a week or two. In both instances, she will have got bored with the games because they have become too simple for her. On an adult level, even a game such as Dungeons and Dragons, whose basic rulebook is more complicated than the average DNA molecule, is not complex enough for some, who must progress to even more sophisticated variants of the game.

I have a fantasy that someone will invent a game so complicated and so fascinating that the entire human race will end up constantly engrossed in it. Civilization will crumble, and the aliens will arrive ready to take over the planet without a shot being fired. All will go well with the invasion, but then some of the crew will come across the Game and give it a try. Panic-stricken by the effects, the alien commanders will pull their fleet off Earth and try to get as far away as possible. In this way, the entire Universe will become 'infected' by the Game, and civilization of every kind will die.

But we are looking too far into the future, and I am digressing – as usual.

A third necessary component of a fascinating game is that it must have some definable objective. In most games, this is winning: one side aims to beat the other. However, in some cases the objective may change during the course of the game: in cricket, for example, one team may score a minor 'win' by successfully batting it out for a draw. In noncompetitive games the definition of the word 'winning' is rather different, but its essential meaning is the same. My wife will draw a lump of wood because she wants to 'win' a better perception of it and, hence, of the Universe at large. I will write a book for an exactly analogous reason – the possibility of gaining fame and fortune being quite secondary (although even quite a small fortune would be much appreciated). Winning in the competitive sense is for some unfathomable reason generally regarded – in Western culture at least – as being somehow more 'respectable'. In the life-game, which is the one we all play, society as a whole smiles upon the competitive approach and is if anything bemused and slightly irritated by the noncompetitive one. In fact, very often the objectives of the latter are very much more worthwhile and, for the 'winner', much more satisfying.

We have, then, three essential components of the partnership between you and a game which fascinates you: (1) You have to understand the basic rules and the essential skills involved, since otherwise you won't be able to recognize good play when you see it. (2) The game must not be so simple that it just bores you or so inflexible that, even if the rules are complicated, there comes a time when the game eventually has given you all the fascination that it can. (3) In some way, you 'win'.

Cricket, for me, qualifies on all three counts. (1) I have an adequate if not especially profound understanding of its basic principles, gained in the ideal way – through playing it (albeit not very well). (2) While the rules of the game are not especially complicated – in comparison with those of Dungeons and Dragons, for example – they allow a very considerable flexibility. No two games are ever identical – indeed, I don't think any two can ever even be very similar – because of factors such as the size of the ground, the weather, individual performances, the state and size of the pitch, the toss, Mrs Jones' Dundee cake, and the sum the opposition have offered the umpires. (3) If playing, I can win if my team wins, or if we draw, or if we lose but have a bloody good match, or if I take a handful of wickets, or if I bat well enough to surpass my career best (a quite spellbinding 27), or even if I take a difficult catch. When playing, then, there are several ways – at both team and individual levels – in which I can come away from the match with what a psychologist would doubtless call something like a 'winning experience'; if you play like I do and for the team I do, this plurality of 'winning' possibilities is very useful. Similarly, when I am merely watching, I can 'win' if 'my' team wins, or if I'm lucky enough to see a real thriller of a match, or some spectacular bowling, batting or fielding performance.

Cricket seems, therefore, to be ideally constructed to fascinate me – and presumably the same is true for you, or you wouldn't be reading this book. It gives our minds those twin essential extramural activities: relaxation and stimulation. It remains fascinating not because any one genius thought up a masterly set of rules, in the way that Clarence Darrow invented Monopoly, but because it has evolved – and still is doing so – and because that evolution has been guided: countless unsung heroes have amended the rules over the years with the precise aim of making the game more and more absorbing. Not all these improvements have been made very deliberately: for example, some useful changes to the rules were made in the wake of the Packer Circus affair of a few years ago, though one gathers that, overall, the whole package of 'Packer rules' produced pretty dull matches. But, whatever their origin, these constant minor amendments ensure that cricket remains a living sport.

Games like cricket fascinate because they can provide the mind's necessary stimulation, at least in part, but why should the mind *need* that (or any other) stimulation? The body certainly needs physical stimulation: the blind, for example, develop compensatingly acute powers of smell, hearing, etc. – look at the way Helen Keller developed a whole world of touch which was astonishingly *visual* in nature. It may be that physical and mental stimulation are really the same thing; again the example of Helen Keller springs to mind. And Robert Ardrey once reported the curious case of some very lowly worms which were subjected to Y-shaped mazes; they were placed at the foot of the 'Y', down one of the branches of which was the reward of some water. After a while, the worms became *apparently* bored (I stress the word 'apparently': one mustn't become too anthropomorphic about worms), and refused to go on trying to solve the puzzle of the maze until one of the experimenters had the bright idea of putting sandpaper along the maze's floor. This gave a nice tickly sensation to any worm that crawled along it, and so the experimental animals began to cooperate once more.

But if physical and mental stimulation are very closely related, they are certainly not identical – we are not, for example, very often at our most intellectual during the act of love. It seems to me that we can identify the area of overlap between the two types of stimulation.

The human brain is divided into two roughly symmetrical halves, linked by a narrow bridge called the corpus callosum. It is widely believed (although to be fair, almost equally widely disbelieved) that the two halves of the brain have different functions – to the extent that, in essence, there are two quite different 'people' living inside each of us. In the left-brain lives the 'me' that is writing these words – my 'conscious ego', to use the Freudian term. In the right-brain lives someone else altogether, and 'I' don't know very much about him. My right-brain is not a very analytical sort of a fellow, being much better at things like intuition and emotional understanding – things which he often has great difficulty in communicating to 'me'. The messages 'I' get from him are rather diffuse – they may take the form of dreams, or sudden hunches, or a general feeling of well-being, so that 'I' can find myself in the position of the person who says: 'I don't know much about art but I know what I like.' For no logical reason which 'I' can discern, looking at a work of art may make me feel good all over: my right-brain is responding to the work of art so powerfully that the whole of me is aware of it.

Where does this tie in? Well, I have been using the term 'mental stimulation' but carefully have refrained from defining it. I do not, in fact, use it to mean 'intellectual stimulation', which term concerns the left-brain only; I use it to mean something rather more. Many of the Dagenham car workers, of whom my aforementioned friend was one, would not have been entranced by a management offer to screen Open University documentaries during the lunchbreak. Many, of course, would have been only too delighted at the prospect of free intellectual stimulation at the company's expense, but many would have preferred a less intellectual form of mental stimulation – a game of football, for example. Both forms of stimulation involve the mind, but one is far more left-brain oriented than the other. Some of the workers might have preferred an art exhibition, some a chamber concert, and so on. Again these are not exclusively intellectual occupations, but they are certainly mentally stimulating. Our reactions to art and music tend to be right-brain – emotional rather than analytical – ones, and they can go on to affect our physical feelings: Bach and Black Sabbath can quite literally make their devotees go weak in the knees, even if in the latter case the devotee will probably go weak in the eardrums first.

So there is a kind of mental stimulation which is distinct from the intellect, and it is possible that what we experience is the cheerful response of the right-brain to the outside stimulus. Of course, the left-brain 'we' don't know quite what is happening or why we are so affected, but this doesn't mean that the reaction doesn't exist. As noted, the right-brain activity laps over both into the physical and into the intellectual regions. Two or more of the three types of reaction may be involved simultaneously and to a similar extent: we may not be intellectual during sex, but clearly *a* mental response is as deeply involved in it all as is our physical one; similarly, devotees of a composer like Mozart or Stockhausen may be both intellectually and emotionally involved at the same time.

In one sphere of activity, however, all three forms of stimulation occur simultaneously. I refer, of course, to certain sports – and, for me, cricket is paramount among these. My body and both parts of my mind are involved in the game; on some noteworthy occasions, all three will even 'sing' together. Outside cricket, this happens to me only rarely; within it, it happens reasonably often.

I'm not making this point as part of some self-indulgent 'confessions of a cricket addict', nor am I trying to do anything so portentous (or, more likely, pretentious) as to produce some wacky 'philosophy of cricket'. What I am saying is that a humble – oh, all right, noble – sport such as cricket can give to the participant plenty of what Abraham Maslow has dubbed 'peak experiences' – those times when your whole mind and body seem somehow to zip into a 'higher dimension' or onto a 'loftier plane'. The aim is much the same as that of some of the oriental mystics: the complete integration of both parts of the mind with the body (and hence with the rest of the Universe).

As I say, at such moments, right-brain, left-brain and body all 'sing' together.

I am not pretending that such experiences encountered by the individual during a cricket match are of profound importance to humanity as a whole: if I were ever to play against Geoff Boycott, and in the unlikely event of my bowling him, it would certainly constitute something of a peak experience for me, but the government would remain untoppled and the laws of science would remain unrepealed. It would be a personal reaction. But that doesn't mean that it would not be significant on the larger scale of things, because of course it would be in quite a different way something which was indeed shared with all humanity: we all need peak experiences from time to time. I would be epitomizing a very important human experience. In other words, while a personal reaction to something is in itself trivial for all but the person involved, it is important on the more global scale because all the rest of humanity has exactly similar peak experiences, albeit in different contexts.

The mental stimulation I have been talking about is,

then, an experience in which, often enough, the right-brain and the left-brain are *both* enjoying themselves. And it is this comparatively rare experience of the two halves of the brain cooperating which is what gives games their importance. Sure, at other times we can have the joy of being stimulated intellectually, emotionally or physically, and sometimes in more ways than one; but games provide us with one of the easier ways in which we can have the feeling that all three aspects of ourselves are being stimulated in concert.

We require the stimulation that games can provide as much as a man in the desert requires water, and for similar reasons: totally deprived of it, we would die. Or, at least, we would no longer be human beings – which is very much the same thing.

Discussing, in theoretical terms, some wild ideas about the fundamental importance of games to the human psyche and hence to the human race may seem a long way from the kind of cricket which I and quite possibly you play. As Roy Hattersley once wrote, it's less a matter of the sweet sound of willow on leather and more one of the sound of a rather sickly snick followed by screams as the slips nurse their staved fingers. However, as I have proposed, cricket possesses the same attraction – the same ability to stimulate and fascinate – at all its levels.

There have been hundreds if not thousands of books telling tales of cricket at the topmost levels. There have been plenty of lengthy written discussions of county cricket, Sheffield Shield cricket, and all the other national equivalents. Village cricket has received a certain amount of attention – usually in glowing terms of long summer evenings and flickering willow, although A. G. Macdonnell in his masterful description in *England, Their England* gave the game away by telling it like it was.

Far, far further down than all of these we have the murky depths of cricket – the kind of cricket *I* play. The kind of cricket, in fact, which *most* cricketers play. However, while the word 'depths' might seem to have derogatory connotations, for the reasons which I have stumblingly put forward I do not think that 'our' kind of cricket is any less important than that played at Test level: it is every bit as important, and in many ways is directly linked. The events on 'our' fields can be every bit as exciting as those at Lord's, the Melbourne Cricket Ground, or either of the Kennington and Kensington Ovals. Moreover, 'our' matches usually contain a far greater amount of amusing incident than do 'theirs'. We are lucky to be playing the kind of cricket we do.

Of course, there can be some overlap between the depths and the first-class game. John Pierce tells of the time when he was playing in an odds'n'sods *vs* Somerset game, put on for some charity or another: he was less delighted that the scorebook showed that he had hit a 4 off Vic Marks than that he'd been clean bowled by Viv Richards – because in some dusty archive their two names will be forever united. Another similar team took on Essex a few years ago, only to be dismissed for a score in single figures. After the embarrassment, the odds'n'sods set up – in an attempt to make it one-all – a drinking contest between their champion, an actor of legendary capacity, and one from the Essex team. To the chagrin of the visitors, Essex won that one, too.

But such direct interactions are rare, and probably to be resisted by lucky cricketers such as ourselves. I am certain that the club I belong to, the West Country Publishers' CC, would decline a membership application from Ian Botham, should it ever arrive: a player of that calibre would destroy any enjoyment we might get from our matches, although it would be nice to be on the

winning side a little more often. No, good matches at our
level – as at every other – require the contesting teams to
be reasonably well matched. They require the genuine
camaraderie that exists between the opponents (often
missing at higher levels), and that camaraderie would
abruptly disappear were we to field a Botham. I have
seen it happen. I have played in a 'friendly' match where
the opposition turned up with three 'ringers' from a
higher level of cricket. I got one of them out by quite
deliberately mentally intimidating the umpire into agreeing with my lbw appeal when the batsman was standing a
foot outside his leg stump, and I felt in no way dishonest
about doing so. I did not feel that I was the one who was
cheating: the opposition had done so by using unfair
tactics.

And that's another aspect of the depths of cricket
which deserves some attention: the general honesty of
the players. It is not uncommon, thanks to television's
action replays, to see cases in Test cricket of batsmen
knowing full well that they were caught behind and yet
staying at the wicket because the umpire failed to notice
the deflection. This sort of behaviour is generally not well
received at 'our' level. All kinds of other curious tactics
may be used – Mrs Jones' Dundee cake – but when
you're out and you know it you 'walk', whatever the
umpire says. In one case when I had been umpiring for
our side, one of our batsmen later told me that he had
indeed been out when I had turned down an appeal, but
had not 'walked': I was furious with him on the grounds
that he made me look dishonest. On another occasion a
member of the opposition boasted about how lucky he
had been that the umpire had failed to give him out, and
was surprised when no one – not even a member of his
own team – seemed very keen to buy him a drink or
accept one from him.

We are gentlemen, we lousy cricketers . . . unless, of course, we're ladies.

Women's cricket receives far too little attention. Test matches between men quite frequently are the subject of front-page coverage in the newspapers, but Test matches between female teams are lucky to be given a brief paragraph among the small ads – if that. There seems to be no logical reason why women's cricket should be any less potentially exciting than men's: as I have said several times, what matters is that the two teams in a game are well matched. There may be no female cricketer capable of bowling as fast as Malcolm Marshall or hitting the ball as hard as Lance Cairns, but that doesn't really matter; and in such fields as spin bowling there is no reason at all why women should not be as adept as – or more adept than – any male counterpart. I hope I have repaired the damage a little by including in this book some of the tales emanating from women's cricket – not necessarily of the top-class variety.

I've included also mention of some of the more curious variants of cricket – not baseball, but some of the less well known ones, whether they are played in distant lands or here in England, where it all started. Also I have a few stories from schools cricket, although that level is really quite a lot higher than our own.

As you can imagine, I have relied on the help of dozens of people in the writing of this book. Those who have generously given me their stories – even if, owing to pressure of space, I have been unable to relay all of their tales to you – are listed on page 235. I cannot begin to express my gratitude to these good people.

In particular, thanks must go to the teams which have tolerated the presence on the field of a certain wayward fast bowler: the two of preponderant note are the West

Country Publishers' CC and the Newtown St Matthews CC. Where members of these teams appear in this book (and sometimes I've transported them from one team into another) they do so under pseudonyms: not only do I want to protect the reputations of the more guilty among my friends, I also do not fancy finding, at every match next summer, that someone has lovingly filled my box with oil of wintergreen.

Finally, my daughter Jane and my wife Catherine must be thanked for tolerating the fact that during the summer they barely see me. The latter must also be thanked for the way in which she makes Dundee cakes for me to take along to matches as a contribution to the teas. These Dundee cakes, of course, bear no relation to the ones supplied by Mrs Jones: *she* works for the opposition.

John Grant

1
THE MENTAL MATCH

1st January to 31st December (inclusive), 1960–

The crowd rose as one to applaud Grant's performance. Urged ahead by his beaming team-mates, he loped easily towards the pavilion, acknowledging the clamour of the multitudes with a modest wave and a shy smile. No doubt, in some radio commentary box somewhere, Bill Frindall would even now be computing the last time that a newcomer to Test cricket had taken all ten wickets in both innings, and scored a carefree double century in between – 10 for 17 in the first innings and 10 for 29 in the second. Rather disappointing, thought Grant, that tally in the second innings: if Fowler and Randall, taking turns on the deep-fine-leg boundary, hadn't let through a couple of snicks for four . . . He made sure his face showed no trace of his disappointment.

As he approached the dressing-rooms a curvaceous brunette with GRANT WILL SHATTER YOUR STUMPS screen-printed on her tight-fitting white sweat-shirt slinked up to him and said . . .

'Wake up, you lazy sod. It's nearly ten o'clock, and your tea's getting cold. Don't forget that Jim's picking you up at half-past.'

'I was just dreaming about you,' I say muzzily. 'You had GRANT WILL SHATTER YOUR STUMPS screen-printed on your tight-fitting white sweatshirt . . .'

'My sweatshirt's in the wash. Don't you remember? You forgot to wash your hands after getting the coal in last night.'

The bruise on my shin begins to throb, as if reminded, and I start to remember all too clearly a drunken urge . . .

Hey, you! Yes, *you*! The reader. Kindly stop eaves-dropping on my private life. Our little domestic discussions are absolutely none of your business. Shove off.

Oh, you're bigger than me? Hmmm, well, that is a point. All right, if you insist on poking your nose into my innermost secrets, I suppose I ought to let you explore all – well, some – of the corridors of my fantasy life. Even Walter Mitty would be staggered and impressed by the scope and scale of my cricketing prowess, as demonstrated to all and sundry only between these walls of bone and scalp.

To tell you the truth, I'm not too terribly embarrassed by your intrusion. Anyone who's ever played cricket – and probably quite a few people who haven't – has a whole repertoire of what I like to call the mental matches. In fact, there are really three different types of mental match – for most of us, at least. Speaking for myself, my mental match in the first category is the one where I open the bowling for England (although, to be honest with you, if the West Indies showed sufficient interest I'd gladly pop over to Barbados and live there long enough to qualify for Test selection). I don't mind if I don't take too many wickets in my Test debut: two or three an innings would be quite enough. All I care about is that my bowling doesn't get hit about too much. I would like at least one of my wickets to be a clean-bowled – just to show that I can do it on my own, without the help of the fielders. Viv Richards, if you want to make an old man very happy . . .

The second type of mental match is rather more plaus-ible. At least, it corresponds to matches in which you are actually going to play. At the end of every season, as you notice that you have taken very few wickets and scored even fewer runs, your mind turns to the matches you're going to play *next* season. At first you're a little gloomy, but by about December you're beginning to think about them with eager anticipation. Oh, boy, are those stumps going to be shattered to matchwood or are they going to be shattered to matchwood? All during those long, frustrating months of the early spring the emotion intensifies, as you practise bowling a tennis-ball against the back of the house, having first made surreptitiously sure that no one's watching. Then come the nets, in April. Your first day out, and you're bowling astonishingly well. Your batting seems to have improved, too: that late cut would have certainly gone for four, and possibly made it for a six (just like David Gower did it on the telly a couple of seasons ago).

The next morning, of course, you are far too stiff and weary to play in any mental matches. The stiffness is perhaps the easier of the two conditions to cope with. Despite the fact that every muscle of your body is screaming its protest, despite the fact that, while you can force yourself agonizingly to climb out of bed and walk those few tortured steps to the lavatory, you find when you get there that you can't sit down – despite all this, as I say, the stiffness causes you less torment than the weariness, born from the 'few drinks' that you and your team-mates had after the net practice. Oh, God, you'll never look a Guinness and Bacardi in the face again . . .

But over the next few days the mental-match cricket season begins in earnest. An old lady cackles when she sees you bowling as you stroll to the shops: does she not realize that, even now, Geoff Boycott is ruefully trudging back to the pavilion, thinking of hanging up his bat for life? All right, all right, it's not really Geoff Boycott, it's that top-notch opener from Wimpole, but the principle's the same.

On the way to the first match of the season, your mind is conjuring up so many fantasy games that it's difficult to see where you're going. Flashing blades of willow . . . balls flying into the cow-field . . . and, later, when you're called on to bat – sorry, no, blast it: that should read 'called on to bowl' – the stumps spread in all directions. Ah, it's going to be one of those days . . .

A few hours later you look back with rather less fondness on being clean bowled first ball and having been hit out of the ground by all and sundry without taking a wicket. But deep in your heart you're already playing the next game – and what a game *that* one's going to be!

The third type of mental match is the one you've already played in. This may sound like something of a contradiction in terms, but it isn't. Mental matches in this category usually start, like Class Two mental matches, in about December of the year in which they were in reality played. Thereafter they will run and run. OK, so in *fact* your bowling was hit happily to the far corners of the ground even by the rabbits, but in your mind the match adopts a rather rosier hue. Think of all those dropped catches! If Rudolph had only been a foot or two taller he'd have held on to at least three! And, although it's gone down in the scorebook as a golden duck that you scored, well, the figures don't tell you everything: you were given out lbw despite the fact that the ball was going *miles* down the leg side, and anyway the sun was in your eyes, you were being attacked by a wasp – or even, as Godfrey once announced to a staggered bunch of us, 'my bat got stuck in the mud'.

The years pass, and everyone else but you forgets what your performance in that match was really like. In fact, so do you: when you talk about how you sent the wickets flying you're no longer telling a lie. You genuinely believe that it happened. Your memory, being a kind-hearted sort of a fellow, has decided to have mercy on you, to make life a little easier for you.

To enjoy all three types of mental match to the hilt, it probably helps to be a writer. Then you can spend the winter months writing about the matches you'd like to play in, that you're going to play in, or that you have played in. To a great extent, this is exactly what I'm doing at the moment. It is a freezing January day; the icy slush on the pavements is as slippery as hell; and I'm wrapped up in about fourteen jerseys and hammering away at the typewriter. And, as I do so, my mind is beginning to wander to the glories that this new season will bring . . .

Writers have had many reasons to create mental matches. Of course, there are many who play or who have played cricket, and therefore find it impossible to resist the temptation to realize their wildest fantasies in print. But others have had other, higher, motives.

Charles Dickens' shortish piece, 'Sunday Under Three Heads', was a straightforward work of propaganda. As he was writing, there were repeated threats from those on high to bring in new laws to circumscribe people's activities on Sundays: in general these fanatics were saying that, if it was fun, you shouldn't do it on a Sunday. The piece is in three sections. The first concerns the way that Sunday actually was: the rich congratulated themselves on their piety in going to church, while the poor could do little but pray for some relief of their miserable lot. This misery would not be alleviated, Dickens suggested in the second section, by the introduction of the proposed Sabbath laws: the Lord's day would be marked not by joy but by gloom.

It is the third section of 'Sunday Under Three Heads' which concerns us, though. In 'As It Might Be Made'

Dickens tries to paint a picture of what Sunday really *ought* to be like – and, despite the efforts of the descendants of those same hyper-Puritan bigots, what it today really *is* like for many of us. The Lord is not best served, Dickens implies, by long, dour faces and a resentment of the Sabbath as twenty-four hours of incomprehensible tedium. No, you can worship God in many ways, and one of them is by enjoying yourself with your fellow human beings. (One is reminded of the tale – where did it come from? – of the mediaeval juggler who was berated by the abbot for juggling and jesting in front of the crucifix. The abbot, wise man, relented when the juggler explained that he was worshipping God by giving to Him of his best.)

Of course, there is no better way of enjoying yourself with your fellow human beings than by playing cricket. (Did I hear a throaty adolescent giggle of disagreement from one of my more puerile readers?) And so we find:

As I approached this spot in the evening about half an hour before sunset, I was surprised to hear the hum of voices, and occasionally a shout of merriment from the meadow beyond the churchyard; which I found, when I reached the stile, to be occasioned by a very animated game of cricket, in which the boys and young men of the place were engaged, while the females and old people were scattered about: some seated on the grass watching the progress of the game, and others sauntering about in groups of two or three, gathering little nosegays of wild roses and hedge flowers. I could not but take notice of one old man in particular, with a bright-eyed grand-daughter by his side, who was giving a sunburnt young fellow some instructions in the game, which he received with an air of profound deference, but with an occasional glance at the girl which induced me to think that his attention was rather distracted from the old gentleman's narration of the fruits of his experience. When it was his turn at the wicket, too, there was a glance towards the pair every now and then, which the old grandfather very complacently considered as an appeal to his judgment of a particular hit, but which a certain blush in the girl's face, and a downcast look of the bright eye, led me to believe was intended for somebody else than the old man, – and understood by somebody else, too, or I am much mistaken.

I was in the very height of the pleasure which the contemplation of the scene afforded me, when I saw the old clergyman making his way towards us. I trembled for an angry interruption to the sport, and was almost on the point of crying out, to warn the cricketers of his approach; he was so close upon me, however, that I could do nothing but remain still, and anticipate the reproof that he was preparing. What was my agreeable surprise to see the old gentleman standing at the stile, with his hands in his pockets, surveying the whole scene with evident satisfaction! And how dull I must have been, not to have known until my friend the grandfather (who, by-the-bye, said he had been a wonderful cricketer in his time) told me, that it was the clergyman himself who had established the whole thing: that it was his field they played in; and that it was he who had purchased stumps, bats, ball, and all!

It is such scenes as this I would see near London on a Sunday evening. It is such men as this who would do more in one year to make people properly religious, cheerful, and contented, than all the legislation of a century could accomplish.

Dickens' point is fairly made, but in fact there have always been a goodly number of enlightened clergymen who have realized that, in itself, a game of cricket provides as 'holy' a way of celebrating the Sabbath as any. Of course, I use the expression 'in itself' because of cricket's rather sordid early history, when the main purpose of the game seems to have been either, at the bucolic level, to injure as many of the opposition as possible, or, at the aristocratic level, as a means whereby vast sums of money could be gambled. No wonder that some of the clergy protested in those days.

But, as I say, many vicars and priests nowadays approve of Sunday cricket – and many, of course, actively take part in it. J. M. Kilburn, in his *Overthrows* (1975), tells several entertaining tales of a team he once played for called the Craven Gentlemen, run by just such a benign pastor, the Reverend C. E. D. Crane. As Kilburn points out, the difficulty of playing for the Craven Gentlemen was that the side frequently included a high proportion of cricketers with whom one had never played before and whose abilities, therefore, were completely unknown to the captain of the day and his other players.

The difficulty was brought home to Kilburn in one game when he was protecting an undistinguished number 11 batsman. Only a few runs were needed for victory, and so survival and the slow garnering of the necessary singles were the order of the day. At the end of one over, Kilburn did the customary thing: he played a stroke while calling for a quick single, in order to keep the bowling. But as he arrived halfway down the pitch he was dismayed to see his partner standing stock-still with a hand cupped to his ear, murmuring: 'I beg your pardon. What did you say?' Nobody had remembered to tell Kilburn that this particular team-mate was deaf!

Kilburn tells, too, of a match the Craven Gentlemen played against St Peter's School, York. The Reverend Crane, having been put in to field, told the rest of the team that, in order to make a game of it, he'd decided to bowl a few gentle overs himself to begin with, so that the school side would at least get off to a good start. What the kind man *didn't* realize was that one of the incoming schoolboys was a certain Norman Yardley . . .

In many other respects, too, Dickens' cricket match is played and replayed all over the land every Sunday. The bashful batsman and his bashful belle . . . well, I know one lower-level cricketer who successfully put an end to the affair his wife was having by both out-bowling and out-batting his youthful rival. After a couple of matches she never looked at the lad again. And, of course, the old man – 'who, by-the-bye, said he had been a wonderful cricketer in his time' – is still with us: for all I know, the old men I see at our matches are the same ones that Dickens saw. Eric N. Simons, another writer known more for his writings not about cricket, talks about these old men in his excellent book *Friendly Eleven* (1950):

Some of them have sight good enough to recognize the players as they emerge from the battered old pavilion; some have not, but would die rather than confess it; and this weakness is respected. A convention has grown up by which those who cannot see say, casually: 'Who's next in?' before the batsman appears. Those who can, wait judiciously until he is just, and only just, visible in the doorway, then remark: 'Ah reckon it'll be Bob,' in the same casual tone. Never, never, with the air of conveying information to the ignorant, but always as if merely prophesying what all will shortly confirm for themselves. The half-blind elders nod their heads wisely, and as the lonely white figure walks to the crease, say: 'Ay, it's Bob, reight 'nuff!' with an assurance they cannot really feel.

Simons, as I say, was known more for his writings on topics other than cricket – indeed, on the title page of *Friendly Eleven*, he is described as 'Author of numerous books of no interest whatsoever to cricketers'. When I knew him, many years ago, it was because I was editing a series of books of his about, of all things, metallurgy. He and his charming wife entertained me to lunch, and as we chatted it became evident to me for the first time that I was talking with the author of, not just some dreary fact-packed books on metal heat-treatment, but of some rather more interesting and literary works. It soon became clear that I was in the company of a minor literary figure who, had history played its cards rather differently, might have become at least a semi-major one. Even so, my jaw dropped slightly when he told me about the time H.G. Wells had approached him with the idea that they should write a book together. He told me the reasons why this had never come about, but I'm afraid I can't remember them. Much more annoyingly, however, he never told me about his passion for cricket.

That was a pity. It was only a few years ago that I came across a reference to his *Friendly Eleven* for the first time. I assumed that the author must be a different Eric Simons – but no, it was the same man. More than anything else I kicked myself for the fact that all these years had gone by without my having made the acquaintance of such a fine book: perhaps more than any other I have read, it captures the 'feel' of low-level British cricket.

In it Simons (as I have done in this book) changes the names of his own team-mates to protect the guilty. The team concerned is the Maye CC, with its various characters who will certainly be recognizable to you: if they don't play for *your* team then you will have played against them countless times. Surely you know Happy Sam the slow spin bowler, who's getting on a bit in years but who, on his day, can get the ball to come in a yard or more; Harry the postman, fast-bowling hero of the local kids and a batsman who, if he gets his eye in, can send the ball all the way over into the next county; Arthur the Wag, who keeps both teams in such stitches that they never notice until afterwards that he's scored really quite a lot of runs . . . Yes, I told you you'd have met them.

Friendly Eleven was published just after the last great war – in fact, internal evidence suggests to me that it was largely written before that conflict – but it is clear from its faithful, accurate portrait of the cricket of its time both that little had changed since Dickens' day and that little has changed since. There's the old umpire George, in whose absolute infallibility everyone (including himself) believes without question until the sad day that he makes a decision so bad that even the fielders appeal to him not to give the batsman out. After a long delay George calls the batsman back: 'Coom back, lad! There's a doubt about it, an' Ah'll gi'e thee t'benefit.' Happy Sam, the demon spin bowler, when fielding can never resist giving the ball some especially vicious tweak as he tosses it back to the bowler (an almost uncontrollable habit of my own: my arm wants to prove that it could make me a great spin bowler if only I'd let it). Harry, the fast bowler, on the other hand, has difficulty in stopping himself throwing the ball at the stumps at about Mach 3: the result is almost always four overthrows. Young Dick is 'the only man I have ever heard lay the blame for being bowled on the distraction of his eye by a white cabbage butterfly fluttering across the pitch'. The heavy roller is so devastatingly heavy that it forces water up out of the ground where no one had ever expected it to exist; the rumour has it that one of the local farmers offered to hire it in place of a water-diviner. There is a fund-raising 'comedy match', at which everyone thinks it's ever-so-ho-ho-hilarious when one of the players bustles around the pitch on a child's tricycle; the author, whose job it is to return the remains of the tricycle to the relevant kid after the match, sees the not-so-funny side of things. There's Young George, who runs between the wickets so enthusiastically that one time, having skied the ball, he collides with a fielder as he desperately tries to take a quick single: a good move, because the fielder staggers off and, in turn, collides with mid-on, who has been waiting to take a simple catch. Every club has memories like these . . .

However, the section of the book that rings most true to me is Simons' description of the Maye CC's pavilion:

Not all that is visible is loveliness, however. There is our pavilion. Once this was a stout, wooden, roomy building; but during the war a great storm took advantage of damage previously done by intruders in quest of loot. With savage fingers it rent loosened plank from plank; tore away one end of the roof with the fury of a hungry husband opening a recalcitrant sardine tin; and even hurled the umpires' coats high into the air, so that for days they hung, flapping spectrally, up a tall tree, whence young Keith eventually collected them.

We were left with half a hut and some widely scattered timber, which disappeared with that amazing rapidity displayed by things left lying about in these none too honest days. When the war was over, we contributed each an odd board from dim recesses of our back-yards; begged some wood from old Josiah, the joiner; had some promised by Darfield, which turned up unfortunately six months too late; and, between us, knocked up a new end on the still standing half.

We were then possessed of a hut, which we fondly refer to now as our 'pavilion'. It is a black and battered old hovel, murky inside, littered during the season with all the impedimenta of a cricket club, leaky about the roof, and inclined to stab you with sharp and icy daggers of air if you strip in it. Hence, all visiting teams who possess normal intelligence dress in the room so thoughtfully (and profitably) provided by 'The Rose and Crown', where there are warmth and comfort, and Old Norman is available to bring you a 'jar' when you need one – two, if you feel like it.

Who, I wonder, was responsible for shipping this 'pavilion' down from Simons' Derbyshire and erecting it in the grounds of . . . but no, I don't want a libel suit on my hands.

On the subject of rustic pavilions, Colin Cracknell of Heston CC tells of the time he played in Balcombe, Sussex, in a lovely ground surrounded by fields full of placidly grazing cows. You can conjure up the picture yourself. What really brought it home to Cracknell that this was one of yer real *rural* matches was his discovery when he came to put on his box: sitting inside it, clearly quite content with the world, was a frog. No doubt it had thought him extremely considerate to have left this nice cool pink plastic armchair so handy for it.

Wells, of course, never wrote that book with Simons,

but I would like to think that it might have been a book on cricket. Before we look at Wells' writing on the game, though, it's worth pausing for a moment to remember that not *all* writers are cricket addicts. In late 1984, for example, I decided to see if one of my vague impressions, that science-fiction writers and readers are not interested in cricket, was correct by asking David Langford, editor of the SF 'newszine' *Ansible*, to put in the next issue a request that any cricket-loving SF people contact me: not one of them did, so I can only presume that my hunch was correct. (I made similar requests to the editors of *Spaceflight* and *New Scientist* concerning my strong hunch that astronomers were more likely to be cricket-lovers than most. The editor of *Spaceflight* wrote back to give me the – perfectly good – reasons why it was a matter of policy that the magazine never ran requests such as mine. The editor of *New Scientist* didn't.)

Ignoring SF authors, though – and, let's face it, most cricketers do – other writers have displayed their stark indifference to the game. George Bernard Shaw on one occasion, on being told that England had just won the Test against Australia, asked innocently: 'What have they been testing?' I get the impression that he was being a 'professional Irishman', deliberately pretending to be ignorant about this 'English' game. His fellow Irishman, novelist William Trevor, writing in *Strangers' Gallery* (edited by Allen Synge, 1974), is a little more honest about his profound hatred for cricket – *playing* cricket, that is; he confesses to more recently spending many an afternoon watching the game at Taunton. He is responsible for having invented a new variant of the game when he found himself

teaching all subjects and all games at a preparatory school. Naturally, the rules of cricket had to be bent. The fast-travelling hard ball was still a danger, and I su[b] tennis ball. I also forbade the use of p[a] they looked absurd, and abandoned th[e] were no overs at all in the games I took, leg-byes, leg-before-wicket, middle-and-l[e] keepers' gloves, or running people out. O[n] tennis ball at the stumps and the boy in fr[o] attempted to strike at it with the bat. If anoth[er] the boy with the bat was out, or if he hit the stu[mps ...] [i]s out: he could not be out in any other way. I had a[b]andoned the business of having overs because it is unnecessary. I abandoned boundaries because all runs should be properly scored, as the word implied, by running. Each boy bowled for a bit and each boy batted. I stood in the same position all afternoon, behind the wicket where the bowler bowled from. I read *The Sittaford Mystery*, *Police at the Funeral*, *Death and the Dancing Footman*, *The Four Just Men*, and *No Orchids for Miss Blandish*.

Were it not for the last of those titles, one might just charitably assume that Trevor was simply one of those people who are more interested in the higher forms of literature than in any such mental activity as cricket. Otherwise, it is completely incomprehensible how he could fail to become instantly enraptured by the game.

Let's get Trevor's foul breath of dissent clear of our lungs by turning to an example of a writer showing quite the opposite approach to the great game. Fictional gunfire might distract Trevor, but even the real thing was barely enough to stop Robert Graves, as revealed in this extract from his famous *Goodbye to All That* (1929):

June 24, 1915. Vermelles. This afternoon we had a cricket match, officers versus sergeants, in an enclosure between some houses out of observation from the enemy. Our front line is perhaps three-quarters of a mile away. I made top score, 24; the bat was a bit of a rafter, the ball, a piece of rag tied round with string; and the wicket, a parrot cage with the clean, dry corpse of a parrot inside. It had evidently died of starvation

...rench had evacuated the town. Machine-gun fire ...p the match.

Filthy Jerry would never learn that, in civilized society, some things just Aren't Done.

Simons' old men, who turn out each and every week to watch the match as best they can, to cackle at great feats or tut at dropped catches, are much loved by the members of the Maye CC. Simons' friend H. G. Wells likewise was interested in the archetypal 'old man of cricket' and wrote about him, but Wells' eyes were far less rosy than Simons', and decidedly far less so than Dickens'. Wells' old man, who appeared in a short piece called 'The Veteran Cricketer' (which you can find in his 1898 collection *Certain Personal Matters*), is a rather unpleasant bore, who 'lives by himself in a small cottage outside the village – hating women with an unaccountable detestation – and apparently earns a precarious livelihood, and certainly the sincere aversion of the country side, by umpiring in matches'.

His umpiring is pedagogic in tone; he fails to see the contest in the game. To him, who has heard his thousands roar as the bails of the best of all England went spinning, these village matches are mere puerile exercises to be corrected. His corrections, too, are Olympian, done, as it were, in red ink, vivid, and without respect of persons. . . . He never uses vulgar bad language himself, but has a singular power of engendering it in others . . . 'Why can't you play without swearing, Muster Gibbs?' he will say, catching the whispered hope twenty yards away, and proclaiming it to a censorious world. And so Gibbs, our grocer and draper, and one made much of by the vicar, is shamed before the whole parish, and damned even as he desired.

The old man, though, reserves much of his spleen for the local vicar, who 'conceives it his duty to encourage cricket by his participation. *Duty* – to encourage cricket!' And Wells sympathizes with his 'veteran cricketer' in this: the vicar is one of those who would be ideal in an urban slum, but is totally out of place in a rural parish, where the priorities of life are just . . . well . . . different. In truth, the antagonism between them arises because of the age-old difference between 'city folk' and 'country folk', and the customary (although not universal) arrogance of the former when confronted by the latter.

Wells' vicar, one of those unfortunates who has been set down in quite the wrong place to serve his parishioners, does his best to blend in with the yokels, as it were, by playing in their cricket team. Whatever the poor fellow does, his participation can't be taken by his parishioners as anything other than patronizing. And, of course, the old man feels this most of all . . .

Then appears our vicar in semi-canonicals, worn 'to keep up his position,' or some such folly, nervous about the adjustment of his hat and his eyeglasses. He approaches the pitch, smiling the while to show his purely genial import and to anticipate and explain any amateurish touches. He reaches the wicket and poses himself as the convenient book he has studied directs. 'You'll be caught, Muster Shackleforth, if you keep your shoulder up like that,' says the umpire. 'Ya-a-ps! that's worse!' – forgetting himself in his zeal for attitude. And then a voice cries 'Play!'

The vicar swipes wildly, cuts the ball for two, and returns to his wicket breathless but triumphant. Next comes a bye, and then over. The misguided cleric, ever pursuing a theory of foolish condescension to his betters at the game, and to show there is no offence at the 'Yaaps,' takes the opportunity, although panting, of asking my ancient if his chicks – late threatened with staggers – are doing well. What would he think if my cricketer retaliated by asking in the pause before the sermon how the vicarage pony took his last bolus? The two men do not understand one another. My cricketer waves the hens aside, and revenges himself, touching his hat at intervals, by some offensively obvious remarks – as to a mere beginner – about playing with a straight bat. And the field sniggers none too furtively. I sympathize with his malice. Cricket is an altogether too sacred thing to him to be tampered with on merely religious grounds . . .

And the old man, like all veteran cricketers – and, as I've said, like cricketers who are not so veteran, too – plays many a mental match. Necessarily, because of his age, these are all of the third type . . . or are they? Does any cricketer ever reach an age when he – or, for that matter, she – stops dreaming about opening the batting or bowling for England? But it's the mental matches of the days of yore that concern Wells:

One legend of his I doubt; he avers that once at Brighton, in a match between Surrey and Sussex, he saw seven wickets bowled by [prodigious spin] in two successive overs. I have never been able to verify this. I believe that as a matter of fact the thing has never occurred, but he tells it often in a fine crescendo of surprise, and the refrain, 'Out HE came.'

Of course, it would be too impolite to challenge the old man on the details of this match. After all, we must allow our elders to entertain fond memories of doughty deeds that never actually happened, or they will, quite rightly, start interfering with our own daydreaming about the prodigious feats we're going to bring off in the future. In our own older days, we will be able to enjoy dangling our grandchildren on our knee and saying: 'Garner was really livid, and bowling like a maniac, but I just tipped him over the top of mid-on and into the crowd. That soon settled him. Bob Willis? Funny you should ask that . . .'

The team for which I play, the West Country Publishers' CC, has only two full-time writers who regularly play for it: Rudolph and myself. Other writers play occasionally, and at least one other of our regulars has written a book or two. Most of the rest of us are involved in publishing in one way or another, though: we have designers, photographers, and so forth. But we have also a loyal band whose jobs are not remotely connected with the printed word. They are in the side because of the club's primary membership qualification (after the fact that you have to pay your subscription): this is that, to qualify for membership, you have to know a publisher. In this way the side is not only strengthened but made more cheerful. Publishing in the West Country tends to be a very incestuous affair, with everyone knowing everyone else, and so the mixed nature of the cricket team serves a valuable function in allowing we who earn our livings through the written word to make bloody good mates among people who have nothing to do with it. As for their part, they tolerate us with a good grace.

And it is very kind of them to do so because, while there seems to be some strong 'positive correlation' between people of the printed word and cricket, this doesn't mean that the literary cricketers are necessarily very proficient at their sport. The point was noted by J. M. Barrie, in writing about the team he ran, the Allahakbarries, in 1930.

Soon it became clear to Anon [Barrie] that the more distinguished as authors his men were the worse they played. Conan Doyle was the chief exception to this depressing rule, but after all, others did occasionally have their day, as when A. E. W. Mason, fast bowler, 'ran through' the opposing side, though one never knew in advance whether he was more likely to send the bails flying or to hit square leg in the stomach. Augustine Birrell once hit so hard that he smashed the bat of Anon, which had been kindly lent him, and instead of grieving he called out gloriously, 'Fetch me some more bats.' Maurice Hewlett could sometimes look well set just before he came out. E. V. Lucas had (unfortunately) a style. Will Meredith would have excelled in the long field but for his way of shouting 'Boundary' when a fast ball approached him. Owen Seaman knew (or so he said) how to cut. Henry Ford was, even more than Tate, an unlucky bowler. Jerome once made two fours. Charles Whibley threw in unerringly but in the wrong direction. You should have seen Charles Furze as wicket-keeper, but you would have had to be quick about it as Anon had so soon to try some one else. Gilmour could at least continue to prate about his five. The team had no tail, that is to say, they would have done just as well had they begun at the other end. Yet when strengthened in the weaker points of their armour, namely in batting and bowling, by outsiders surreptitiously introduced, they occasionally astounded the tented field, as when by mistake they challenged Esher, a club of renown, and beat them by hundreds; an Allahakbarrie (whose literary qualifications I cannot remember) notching a century. Anon never would play Esher again, though they begged him to do so almost on bended knee.

Perhaps the most telling comment on the Allahakbarries' skills came from one of their most devoted followers, 'Madame de Navarro'. In one match, when the Allahakbarries were batting on despite having already won the match, Barrie explained to her that there was no need for her to spectate any longer: the game was really over. She doubted his confidence. 'Yes, but you have still several men to go in,' she pointed out sweetly.

However, as Barrie noted, not all of the Allahakbarries were of a uniformly low standard. The major exception was Arthur Conan Doyle, whose renown today rests largely on his most famous creation, Sherlock Holmes, although a few decades ago he was widely known too for his historical novels and his science fiction. (Note that he was one of the few exceptions to the rule about SF writers.) An unusual tribute to his cricketing skills is probably to be found in the fictional creation of Raffles, 'the Amateur Cracksman', by Doyle's friend and brother-in-law, E. W. Hornung.

Like Doyle, Hornung was mad about cricket – despite the fact that he had certain natural disadvantages: his eyesight was poor and he suffered from asthma. He managed to turn himself, however, into a useful middle-order batsman and slow bowler. (He became a member of the MCC in 1907.) Since his creation, Raffles, was a devastating batsman and the best slow bowler in England, it is tempting to think that his cricketing capabilities and exploits represent Hornung's version of the mental match of the first kind. But a rather different interpretation is suggested by one of Barry Perowne's more modern Raffles stories, in which Conan Doyle makes his appearance: Raffles recognizes that here he has found not only his mental but his cricketing master. Whether, therefore, Hornung based Raffles-the-cricketer upon himself or upon his brother-in-law becomes an intriguing question.

Doyle was good: there cannot be any doubt about that. In fact, he was really too good to feature in this book. Even W. G. Grace did not consider Doyle to be a complete buffoon on the cricket field – a wise move, since at least once Doyle took the Doctor's wicket. Moreover, while playing on the same side as Grace at Lord's, he once scored a century.

He was an all-round sportsman: he played football into his forties, and he cycled, ballooned, fished, boxed, hunted (although he later rejected this as the barbaric practice it is), played bowls and billiards . . . He was far from being the shy ascetic which people often assume he was, transferring Holmes' personality onto that of his creator. Most people assume that Doyle was spare and tall, like Holmes, but this was far from the case: he was a beefy fellow, more like Watson than like the 'Great Detective'.

He seems first to have discovered cricket as a schoolboy at Stonyhurst, the Jesuit public school where he spent some years. True, cricket at Stonyhurst was not quite the sort of game that you found at Lord's: the pitch was a stretch of gravel, the bats were unrecognizable, and the bowling was only underarm. In many other ways, though, the game was much the same. A few decades ago, most schools played rounders, a vastly inferior form of both cricket and baseball: nevertheless, there must have been countless cricketers who first discovered the 'real' game through rounders, and the same sort of thing seems to have been true with Doyle.

Whatever the case, his curious introduction to the game certainly does not seem to have stunted his talent. He even represented Britain once – in a tour to Holland. At a rather less formal level, in 1900, while on ship to South Africa, he organized cricket matches on deck: these lasted until the passengers' only cricket ball was lost overboard. A devotee of spiritualism – when he died he left behind him the promise (as yet unfulfilled) that he would do his best to send back a message from the afterlife – at one séance he believed that he had contacted the spirit of a fellow cricketer who had died under Kitchener.

Cricket, in short, was an extremely important part of his life. Charles Higham, one of his many biographers, believes that for at least part of his life Doyle used cricket (and golf) as some kind of sex-substitute. In 1896 he found himself married to a woman whom he loved, but who had tuberculosis and who was therefore, according to the science of the time, sexually *verboten*. At the same time, he was madly in love with the woman who was later to become his second wife, Jean Leckie, but the two had agreed to forgo becoming lovers so long as his first wife should live. A highly honourable decision, but one which must have put him in sexual torment: he was sexually frustrated on two fronts simultaneously. It is hardly surprising that, until his first wife's death in the summer of 1906 (and his subsequent marriage to Jean Leckie in autumn, 1907), he played a lot of cricket in order to sublimate his sexual energies.

His sole cricketing story is a beauty. Published in 1928, only a couple of years before Doyle's death, 'The Story of Spedegue's Dropper' concerns an eponymous hero who devises a brand-new slow-bowling technique: if you send the ball high enough and accurately enough, the batsman will find himself having to defend his wicket not against a ball coming (essentially) horizontally towards it, but against one dropping vertically down upon it. Spedegue is – naturally – called in to save England from crisis and, after much tension, does so. It is a pity that Doyle's brother-in-law, the would-be great slow bowler E. W. Hornung, did not live to read the tale; he had died in 1921.

Doyle treasured his great cricketing moments. After he had married Jean Leckie, the couple bought a house called Windlesham; in fact, Doyle was so badly diddled in the purchase that the house was immediately rechristened 'Swindlesham'. In the hall of this house, where everyone could admire it, hung a muddy bat: it was with this bat that he had scored his maiden century at Lord's. He celebrated the capture of Grace's wicket in more public style even than this – in verse.

> Once in my heyday of cricket
>   Oh day I shall ever recall!
> I captured that glorious wicket,
>   The greatest, the grandest of all.
>
> Before me he stands like a vision,
>   Bearded and burly and Brown,
> A smile of good-humoured derision
>   As he waits for the first to come down.
>
>   · · ·
>
> Well, here goes! Good Lord, what a rotter!
>   Such a sitter as never was dreamt;

It was clay in the hands of the potter,
   But he tapped it with quiet contempt.

The second was better – a leetle;
   It was low, but was nearly long-hop;
As the housemaid comes down on the beetle
   So down came the bat with a chop.

    . . .

The third was a gift, or it looked it –
   A foot off the wicket or so;
His huge figure swooped as he hooked it,
   His great body swung to the blow.

Still when my dreams are night-marish,
   I picture that terrible smite,
It was meant for a neighbouring parish,
   Or any old place out of sight.

But – yes, there's a but to the story –
   The blade swished a trifle too low;
Oh wonder, and vision of glory!
   It was up like a shaft from a bow.

    . . .

Good Lord, was it mine! Such a soarer
   Would call for a safe pair of hands;
None safer than Derbyshire Storer,
   And there, face uplifted, he stands.

    . . .

Out – beyond question or wrangle!
   Homeward he lurched to his lunch!
His bat was tucked up at an angle,
   His great shoulders curved to a hunch.

Walking he rumbled and grumbled,
   Scolding himself and not me;
One glove was off, and he fumbled,
   Twisting the other hand free.

Did I give Storer the credit
   The thanks he so splendidly earned?
It was mere empty talk if I said it,
   For Grace was already returned.

This is not great poetry, perhaps – more of an exultant chant. No doubt Doyle felt that he had drained himself of poetry about the incident out there on the cricket pitch. Bowling the ball that dismissed Grace was enough by way of poetry for any cricketer . . .

A few months ago I was sitting in the pub with Jonathan, probably the member of our club whom I see most regularly, and he suddenly changed the subject of the conversation (probably from women). 'I found out something interesting about Manaton Cricket Club the other day,' he said.

'Oh, yes,' I replied, without much interest. I knew that one of our team played more often for Manaton than for us, and that the village lay somewhere down in the Newton Abbot direction, but that was about it.

'Do you know who founded it?' said Jonathan.

'No . . .' I replied, trying to seem more forgetful than ignorant.

'John Galsworthy,' he said, and then he deftly turned the conversation back to the sleek young blonde who had just arrived in the pub.

Sooner or later, thanks to this tip, I found myself in the excellent West Country Studies Library, in Exeter, finding out a little more about Galsworthy's cricketing activities.

He seems to have developed his love for the sport – in fact, for sports in general – at Harrow. He appears to have been a pretty useful cricketer (and an outstanding footballer). In later years, he made great efforts never to miss the annual Eton *vs* Harrow match at Lord's, frequently bemoaning Harrow's losses. In a way, though, he was truly to rediscover cricket when he was in his fifties and living by Manaton, in Devon. In his wife Ada's hand, but presumably dictated by him, we find the following record of the summer of 1921:

The feature of that summer was the introduction of village cricket. I the veteran member of the team and president. Mostly responsible for scores of 1 and 3, but made 20 against Moretonhampstead, to the considerable astonishment of all present; and 15 in the last match of the season.

His enthusiasm for the new club could not be disguised. Whether, as Catherine Dupré suggests, he became active in Manaton CC simply because, as a now wealthy and famous writer, he wanted to contribute to and be a part of his adopted community (rather like Wells' cleric), or whether – as seems more likely to me – he simply rediscovered and once more fell in love with the sport which he had played in his youth, makes no difference. He was as keen as mustard. He ignored the protests of those of his friends who said he was too old for such violent exertion, and that, with his poor eyesight, the whole affair was dangerous anyway. He turned out for Manaton as one of the players – escaping, for a while, from the shackles of auctorial fame. To his friend Rudolf Sauter he wrote in August, 1921:

Prepare for cricket and bring flannels and shoes. There's a match on Saturday in which I've engaged you to play, and probably a practice on Friday evening. No need for anxiety, you cannot be worse than most of us. Yesterday we played Moreton[hampstead] and thumped them. We made 119 to their 63. And what do you think? I made the equal top score of 20, by a combination of luck and will-power seldom beheld. I counted my runs like a miser, and hang me if the village scorer did't [*sic*] put down a 4 hit, as a 4 *bye*, and made me look to have made a paltry 16. Now, if that wasn't awful at my time of life I don't know what is!

Galsworthy had all the hallmarks of a true low-level cricketer. He modestly claimed, in his letter to Sauter, that he had scored no more than a single for nineteen years – a lie, since occasionally he'd made a little more (2 or 3). But this apparent modesty is counterbalanced by the fact that it was obviously *very important to him* that he had made a score of 20: it's in his letter to Sauter, and it's in his informal record of the summer. To him, it was a memorable feat, and this is the sign of the truly low-calibre player. It is for an exactly analogous reason that my trusty editor has had to go through the manuscript of this book deleting the multiple references to the times when I scored 27 (including a 6), or took 4 wickets for 8 runs, or scored 15 out of a team total of 32, or . . .

And, like me – and almost certainly like you – Galsworthy was keen to practise with whomsoever he could persuade to join in. I practise on the back lawn with my seven-year-old daughter. Galsworthy practised on his, according to his god-daughter, Dorothy Ivens (née Easton), with his wife, Ada, C. S. Evans (from his publisher, Heinemann) and in due course with Dorothy herself. In fact, Heinemann were all too keen to indulge their favourite bestselling author in everything, including cricket: for a while there was an annual match between Heinemann and a John Galsworthy XI, and one year a Heinemann staff-member was nearly sacked for clean-bowling the author. (It may be that Galsworthy himself intervened to prevent this shocking dismissal: he was a sportsman, for one thing, and rejected the idea that he should display *prima donna* tantrums, for another.)

But those friends of Galsworthy's who had warned him about his poor sight and his advancing years were to be, sadly, proven right. In 1923, during a practice session, he was struck hard over the heart by the ball. You or I, on getting this kind of injury, might merely lie down in the middle-distance and gasp for a while; we might show the bruise, and its dramatic coloration as it faded, to our spouses over the next few days; but for Galsworthy it was all rather more serious: he was in poor health for a while. Here are some extracts from his letters of the time:

Dearest Dorothy [Easton]: . . . I'm so glad you're having a cricket success. You will become a kind of fairy godmother, and immortalizer of Kentish cricket.

Here we've had some good games. Beat Bovey Tracey Junior, and Moretonhampstead, and got beaten by Newton YMCA. I wish straight bowling didn't paralyse me. On Friday my cricket week begins. At present I seem to have quite a crop of little ills, so what I shall be like after it I don't know . . .

My cricket week is bust. I got a knock at practice and have been laid up. Nothing to worry about, but enough to stop my playing. So here we are still. We may or may not come up about Thursday, but only for a perch at G.L., because if we do come up I at least must go to [J. M.] Barrie's for the week-end . . .

Things weren't much better when he wrote again to Dorothy Easton at the end of August, 1923:

. . . I am much better these last three or four days. In fact, if only my temp. would cease to go up at about 6.30 for three or four hours, I should be down and out. But the other symptoms are clearing up well, and I feel much more myself. The temperature does linger on in these cases . . .

A couple of days later he wrote to Harley Granville-Barker:

I've been toying with what some calls [*sic*] Cystitis, others Pyeritis, others Nephritis – anyway something lingering and unpleasant, which has only become quietitis in the last two days. To-day I'm down – my temperature having ceased to vibrate, with other signs of clearance. But I'm weak, and got to guard against chills and so forth . . .

The final surrender came in a letter to Dorothy Easton of about the same time. Galsworthy confessed:

> . . . I progressed rapidly till last Thursday afternoon, then had a little set-back from which I'm pulling up again – a nuisance, the whole thing, and the end, I'm afraid, of cricket for me. Well, it was foolish, at my age. Manaton has won 5 out of the last 7 matches . . .

So ended Galsworthy's twilight infatuation with cricket. This major illness was to convince him that he was too old to take part even in this most genial of sports. Ten more years were to pass before his death; perhaps they would have been ten happier years had he realized that sports injuries can happen to anyone, whether 15 or 55. But he had made his decision.

Manaton, by the way, is still a flourishing cricket club. You can go and see it play any weekend during the season. Most of the players don't realize that the club's founder was the great John Galsworthy – and, come to that, why should they? A famous author he might have been, but in cricketing terms he was nothing more than a rather rich man who took the opportunity of his wealth and his position to create a cricket club. Plenty of famous people have done that. One of the great glories of cricket is that such details do not matter: on the cricket pitch the great author, the television star, the journalistic personality, the rock hero – all have no more kudos than the village blacksmith, or plumber, or writer, or coalman, or postman, or friend.

Or, for that matter, poet.

It comes as something of a surprise that John Keats was a keen cricketer (although his favourite spectator sport was boxing) from his schooldays onwards. One's image of him is much more of someone who spent the whole time lounging around in bed being pale and interesting in all directions. In fact, both mental pictures are correct: he was a sort of sporting namby-pamby – as revealed in an excellent essay in *The Twelfth Man* (ed. Martin Boddey, 1971) in which Robert Gittings puts forward the thesis that much of the inspiration behind two of Keats' better known poems came from his playing of the game.

On 18 March 1819, Keats was playing cricket on Hampstead Heath when the ball struck him on the eye – pretty painful, even though it seems that the ball they were playing with was a softish one. The following day, in true Keatsian fashion, he decided to lie moaning abed, using, as he was honest enough to admit in a letter to his brother, his black eye as an excuse to play invalid. In this letter to his brother he goes on to describe the various thoughts that were coursing through his head as he lay there: 'Neither Poetry nor Ambition, nor Love have any alertness of countenance as they pass by me: they seem rather like three figures on a greek vase – a Man and two women – whom no one but myself could distinguish in their disguisement.' As Gittings points out, this *must* have been the origin of Keats' 'Ode on Indolence', especially since Keats had confessed that it was really indolence, rather than his injury, which was keeping him in bed. Here's the relevant bit:

> One morn before me were three figures seen,
> With bowed necks, and joined hands, side-faced;
> And one behind the other stepp'd serene,
> In placid sandals, and in white robes graced;
> They pass'd, like figures on a marble urn . . .

And in due course the three figures are identified as Poetry, Ambition and Love.

The other poem concerned is the famous 'Ode on Melancholy', in which two of the stanzas seem to display imagery which had occurred to Keats on that black-eyed morning (an example of shining inspiration?). However, the relationship is less direct, and it is perfectly possible that the imagery was, as it were, floating around in Keats' mind anyway, surfacing both in his letter to his brother and in the poem. But it is deliciously tempting to maintain that at least part of the poet's inspiration was born from his failings, in this instance, as a cricketer.

However famous or wealthy we are, we can all play just as badly as each other.

So, as it happens, Catherine hurries me out of the house on time and I'm picked up on the corner by Jim, at exactly half-past ten. As the car thrums along the road from Exeter towards Abbotskerswell, both of us, quite consciously and with the other's knowledge, play a few mental matches of the third kind; underneath, of course, we're playing mental matches of the second kind: we know, both of us, that *we're* going to be the people whose dazzling play will lead to a famous victory. (At the same time, we know that our side's going to get stuffed, but our subconscious minds refuse to admit this possibility.)

'I've had this really funny morning,' I say after a while.

'What do you mean?' says Jim.

'Well, it seems there are a hell of a lot of writers – far more than you'd expect there to be – who've been involved in cricket. Most of them have played it; most of them have played it as if it were a way of life, blast it; but even those who haven't played it seem to have treated it as a sport rather different from the other sports. They've either raised it on a pedestal or they've taken it as a sort of *symptom* of the British way of life.'

'OK,' says Jim, 'so yer average particle physicist isn't a cricket freak. Does that mean anything?' (He's a radio DJ, which explains some of his, er, charming patois.)

'Yes, it means that I, a pretty goddam minor writer, really ought to be writing something about the sport which I love.' I look out the side window and see a bull tupping a cow: in the Big City it would be scandalous; down here it's something to be mildly pleased about. 'The trouble is that all the bloody cricket books have been written! It seems like every Test produces a wall-to-wall library. I never see cricket like that: all I ever see is the kind of grot stuff you and I play.'

Jim turns to me with a smile. 'You know,' he says, 'there's a book in that.'

Part One
1983

2
THE TORQUAY MATCH
7th April, 1983

'It's useless,' I say. 'We might as well forget the whole thing and stop at the nearest pub.'

Patrick, who is driving, says nothing at all, just stares ahead into the billowing fog and concentrates on following the dimly glowing rearlights of the car in front. We're chugging along at a steady fifteen miles an hour or so, which is about twice as fast as we ought to be going in these conditions. The fog is white, sinister and dense: the twin cones of the headlights (thank God the nearside one's started working again) stretch out in front of us for only about twenty yards. I swiftly calculate that, at the rate we're going, we should reach the pitch by around seven o'clock, half an hour late. To make it all worse, the occasional glimpses we have of the roadside fields show that some of the weekend's snowfall still remains, frozen solid to the surface of the soil in hard, rocklike clumps.

'There'll be no one else there,' I say. 'Let's find a pub.'

'How the hell do you expect us to find a pub in this weather?' comments Godfrey from the back seat.

The conversation – such as it was – wilts and dies as we all concentrate on trying to pick out roadsigns in the mists ahead of us. Somewhere along this stretch, we think, we have to take a left-hand turn to lead us onto the back road into Torquay. And there it is! Fortunately there's nothing behind us as Patrick reverses a few yards and then accelerates back up to fifteen miles per hour. 'Take it easy,' says someone. 'There's hardly room for two abreast along here.'

'I know the road,' grunts Patrick. The relevance of the

remark escapes me; the reassuring red lights in front have gone. Always a nervous passenger, I concentrate on mental arithmetic for a while.

Surprisingly enough, though, we arrive safely at the pitch, the King George IV ground on the outskirts of Torquay. It's reassuring to see that several cars have arrived ahead of ours – even more reassuring not to be able to recognize some of them, which means that at least a few of the opposition have turned up. There's nothing more embarrassing than to find yourself at a 'foreign' pitch only to discover that your opponents have cancelled the match and forgotten to tell you about it.

The King George IV ground is not, to put it tactfully, one of the country's finest. Dogs are allowed to roam it freely, so that fielding can be hazardous – there's a definite reluctance on everybody's part to go for those dramatic, rolling one-hand catches. Moreover, the ground's a very *ugly* one, for some reason I've never quite been able to pin down: a single glance at it is enough to make you look forward to the moment when you're changing back into your ordinary clothes. To add to the pitch's general undesirability, it's laid out on the side of a hill, so that it's perfectly possible to 'score' a leg-bye boundary past the square-leg umpire.

All of these comments are of purely academic interest this evening, though: the fog is still so thick that, from where we now stand near the changing-rooms ('pavilion' would be far too grand a word), it's quite impossible to see the pitch.

In any other circumstances the match would be called off instantly. However, this is the fourth fixture on our season's list, and the preceding three have all had to be cancelled owing to rain and/or snow. The players who've arrived to represent both sides – nine from ours and eight from theirs – are champing at the bit. Three weeks have gone by since the last of our pre-season net-practices, and some of the more illustrious players are beginning to worry that they might have lost their form. Our opening batsman, a Geoff Boycott fan who has never been known to raise a bat in anger, even in a ten-over thrashabout to pass the time on a Sunday evening until the pubs open, stares at the roiling mists in the direction of the pitch and curses in a low, steady monotone. The bowlers, myself included, start bowling an ancient, tattered practice ball against the rusty brick wall of the changing-rooms; someone slips on a dog-turd and ignominiously misses the changing rooms altogether, so we leave him trying to find the ball in the shrubbery beyond and go back to where the captains are conferring.

'We'll play,' says Godfrey, our skipper, eager to avoid lynching.

'You're on,' says the opposition's captain, 'but we'll have to have some special rules.'

One of the distinctive features of the depths of cricket is to be found in the definition of the expression 'bad light'. Test and county matches are brought abruptly to a halt every time a sparrow flies across the sun; but in *real* cricket the players are made of sterner stuff. Not for them the pusillanimity of the professional namby-pambies – oh, no. Would a professional have played, for example, in the match to determine the destination of the 1982 David & Charles Challenge Trophy?

David & Charles, the publishing company, used to have a cricket team which, in the normal way of these things, was forced to recruit players from outside the company in order to have a chance of producing a full eleven at every match. The crunch probably came when David & Charles took on the nearby publishing firm of Webb & Bower, and found that there were actually more regular David & Charles players in the opposing side

than in the home team itself. The eventual result was the
formation of the West Country Publishers' Cricket Club.

The trophy, however, remains. It is awarded annually
to the victors of a hard-drinking needle-match between
the publishers, on the one hand, and, on the other, a
team made up of journalists from a brace of sister-
newspapers, the *Western Morning News* and the *Exeter
Express & Echo*. Almost by definition, the team which
wins the drinking contest beforehand loses the cricket
match; however, thanks to post-match carousings, they
have a chance of regaining their lost pride in the exceptionally dangerous darts match which may follow.

In 1982 the game was played on a Sunday at the ground
belonging to the Abbotskerswell Cricket Club – a ground
which features with some regularity in these pages. This
resembles Torquay's King George IV ground in being
laid out on a hill, but it is very much smaller and – more
important – has a licensed clubhouse. It is also a ground
with very lovely surroundings, albeit hazardous ones. On
one side there is a field full of cows, so that people who
hit sixes are definitely not popular. It's worse on the
other, I gather: the owner of that property has taken
to challenging cricketers searching for lost balls with a
shotgun.

The plan on this particular occasion, according to one
informant (other informants have given different versions
of it all), was that the two teams should meet at the
clubhouse at about half-past one for a few drinks so that
they might get to know each other; the match was to start
at half-past two, and afterwards there was to be an open-
air barbecue and a few more drinks until the trophy had
been presented; then the wiser souls would make their
erratic way home while most of the players went to the
nearby 'Two Mile Oak' to play darts and . . . well . . .
have a few drinks.

Quite a few drinks, all told.

The first part of the plan went well. By the time the bar-staff arrived at half past one a queue was forming. Soon the drinks were flowing freely. Some of the cricketers thought that it was for this reason alone that things were beginning to seem a bit murky; but no, the sky had genuinely filled with dark, ominous clouds. Nevertheless, at 1425 the umpires went out to inspect the pitch, planted the stumps, and declared themselves satisfied. The two captains tossed a coin, and (I believe) the journalists' early-order batsmen began to pad themselves up.

Just then, the heavens opened.

Reluctantly, the bar-staff shut up shop, promising to return at seven o'clock. Aghast, the cricketers looked at each other. The weather could clear at any moment, so there was no question of immediately calling the match off; but the Abbotskerswell clubhouse, for all its amenities, is a small one, and the prospect of twenty-two full-grown men, plus numerous camp-followers of various sexes, having to spend a few teetotal hours in it making small talk was not a pleasant one.

Then someone had an inspiration. For some reason which I have been unable to establish, it seems that there had been plentiful supplies of wine laid on – presumably these were for the post-match barbecue. On the other hand, since by the time the barbecue began the bar would be open again, did it make any sense not to drink the wine now? Of course it didn't . . .

Unfortunately, the rain continued to pour down. Every hour or so the umpires would grab their umbrellas and paddle unsteadily out to examine the pitch; each time they returned with really quite convincingly gloomy faces and said that, yes, they'd have another. Thunder cracked and lightning flashed, but they supplied no more than a backdrop to what had developed into a memorable (or, even better, totally unmemorable) party. And, just as the wine was beginning to run out, who should turn up but the bar-staff, ready and eager to start selling beer again. The barbecue was forthwith set up in a Dutch-barn-like shelter adjoining the clubhouse. Before any of the participants had any time to realize what was happening, they were all agreeing among themselves that burnt meat was absolutely delicious.

Then, at nine o'clock, the rain stopped as decisively as it had started. The skies cleared as the last rays of the setting sun twinkled and died; a full moon gazed benevolently down on the scene. In short, as somebody pointed out – and no one now admits responsibility – apart from the fact that it was almost completely dark, it was perfect cricketing weather. A bit wet underfoot, but . . .

So began one of only two matches I've ever heard about that have been played in the dark. The other one was played in 1973, when two teams decided to raise money for charity by playing for a solid twenty-four hours at Parker's Piece in Cambridge. All told, there were ten innings, containing between them 367 overs and a grand total of 1395 runs. After the match, thanks to generous contributions from the New Zealanders, who were touring the country at the time and who had watched part of this marathon game, over £150 was raised for the mentally handicapped.

Our players at Abbotskerswell had no such lofty motives, however: all they wanted was a game of cricket. Because it was late and the light was agreed to be 'rather poor', certain new rules came into force. Each side was restricted to ten overs, one from each member of the fielding side (excluding the wicket-keeper); and no bowler was allowed to take a run-up longer than a hop, a skip, and a jump. The umpire at the bowler's end was to be the one holding the torch someone had dug out; even though he thereby had better seeing conditions than his colleague at square leg (who was having to make do with a domestic candle stuck into the top of an empty wine bottle), he was not allowed to give any lbw decisions. Catches behind the wicket were likewise disallowed: since catches in the deep were improbable, to say the least, this effectively meant that the only way in which a bowler could take a wicket was to hit the stumps. (Let's face it, that's by far the best way to take a wicket, anyway.)

Hitting the stumps, though, was not particularly difficult. While the countryside is open towards the western end of the Abbotskerswell pitch, where the last few vestiges of the sun's afterglow were still lightening the sky, at the eastern end there is a row of tall, dark trees. From this end, then, any bowler was to the batsman merely a moving grey patch in the murk, and the delivered ball was totally invisible. The batsman could either stand four-square in front of the stumps, hoping for byes or leg-byes, or attempt to hit the ball into the middle distance – which latter, naturally, most did.

When the blind play cricket they do so with a large, soft ball which makes a noise as it is bowled: the batsman can, therefore, estimate its position at any moment from the grunts of the bowler, the 'thwock' as it hits the ground at a certain distance from him, and so forth. The batsmen at Abbotskerswell were not so fortunate. Apart from the gloom, they had to cope with the dazzling glare of the umpire's torch, shining straight into their eyes. The bowlers barely grunted, having been told by their respective captains to 'take it easy, lad'. The ball hit the muddy ground with a uniformly uninformative 'splotch'. Batting was like trying to swat a moth in a darkened room: you see the target only at the very last moment, and make contact only if you have excellent reflexes.

The scores were, for obvious reasons, not officially recorded, although the umpires did their best to keep a vague tally and the individual batsmen made claims which were greeted, on their announcement in the pavilion, with general mockery. At the end of ten overs it was popularly agreed that the *Western Morning News* team had scored something between 20 and 30, most of them in extras – although wides were, under the circumstances, disallowed. A lengthy 'tea interval' was called for, and then the publishers fumbled their way into their pads.

In the mean time, the children of both sides had decided to emulate the television crowds and mob the pitch. Here, there and everywhere, tennis balls were being merrily lost or tripped over. The bowling creases were being reduced yet further towards a swampish, slithery state by scuffed school shoes. ('Oh, my God, I've got to have those clean by seven in the morning,' came a mother's plaintive wail.) Unfortunately, the invading hordes refused to leave the pitch as the cricketers came in: they abandoned the strip itself, but that was as much as they were willing to concede.

This situation severely circumscribed the publishers' batting and therefore, had all other things been equal, might have won them the match. By this time, of course, the only light left to bat in was moonlight – the sun had long since departed completely. While it was in theory feasible that you might be able to see the ball bowled from the western end in the instant before it hit your stumps, at the other end it was totally impossible. After an over or two, the umpires declared. It was, they protested, unfair to expect them to decide whether or not the ball had hit the wicket – after all, it was perfectly possible that the keeper was stepping forward deftly to remove the bails. Moreover, because of the kids, had any batsman actually hit the ball with one of those exuberantly mighty swings, the results could have been fatal.

The result was, then, a draw. The trophy was shared. Since the trophy and its presenter had, wisely, decided to stay at home, the shared honours were purely abstract. But the bar had not yet quite run dry . . .

It wasn't, they now tell me, quite like that. Even my original informant has begun to doubt some of the details. Others who were there say that there wasn't *that* much drink about. But then all the best cricketing stories exist in several versions – and the match was certainly played, as I have described, in the dark.

Here on the King George IV ground, the conditions are not quite as bad as pitch-black – at least, that's what we tell ourselves as we troop out onto the wicket. Surprisingly, it's in not too bad a condition: a bit soft, maybe, but certainly not unplayably so. The umpires check that it is actually possible to see from one end of the strip to the other, and then Godfrey is dispatching us all to our various fielding positions. I'm planted in a sort of widish mid-on position; as with most of the rest of the team, this means I don't have to change around at the end of each over, but can spend half the time lurking in an uneasy no-man's-land between deep gully and cover point. This is sensible: the fog is now so bad that, were I to attempt to change ends, there'd be a very good chance of my getting lost en route. The only problem is that I can't see what's happening on the strip – and nor can I see any of the other fielders. I realize with singular dread that there's a very good chance of my being struck amidships by a firmly driven ball before I know that the match has even started.

Fortunately, this ultimate disgrace is not to be my lot. One of the umpires considerately shouts 'Play!' into the surrounding mists so that we all know that the first ball is about to be delivered. As you might expect, it's been decided beforehand that no fast bowlers are to be used – on the principle that, should the ball go straight through both batsman and wicketkeeper, it might never be rediscovered. This means, folks, that I'm not going to be given a bowl.

Keen followers of Test cricket have discovered that the ideal way of watching it – apart from actually being at the Oval, or wherever – is to have the television turned on but with the sound off, the commentary being provided instead by BBC Radio's 'Test Match Special' team. This way you can not only see what's going on but also have a full description of it, in case your eyes are deceiving you; moreover, you gain release from some of the more vapid outpourings of the television commentators. (During a 1982 Test match, one of them, Jim Laker, was heard to remark of the 'Nelson', the score 111: 'You know, it's funny how often something seems to happen when the score is 111.') I'm in a situation diametrically opposite to that of the tv-with-radio user: not only can I not see anything of the game but there's no one nearby to tell me what's happening. I jump up and down from time to time, try to deduce from the muffled grunts and thumps that reach me through the pillowish white mist what's going on, and wonder idly if there's a decent pub in the vicinity.

This goes on for quite a while – the jumping, listening and thirsting. After some time I notice that only the jumping and the thirsting are still going; there's a curious silence from the direction of the wicket. I stop jumping and listen carefully: still nothing.

It's almost as if there were no one there . . .

On the way back to the changing-rooms I pass our opening batsmen, padded up and coming in to do battle.

'Oh, hello John,' says Geoff, he of the startling vocabulary (yes, even his Christian name is the same as that of his hero: I wonder if he got it changed by deed-poll?), 'we were wondering where you'd got to.'

I join the rest of the team, who are sitting disconsolately on various items of cricketing equipment – pads, bats, cricketers. 'What's the score?' I ask.

'They got 27, all out,' says Godfrey. I wonder how the hell anyone knows. Even though the scorer was, by prior arrangement, standing next to the square-leg umpire, it must have been pretty hard to work out what was going on.

'27 isn't too bad, in these circumstances,' says Godfrey dolefully. He's quite right: I've played in matches in which, even under the hot summer sun, 27 seemed an impossible target. In *real* cricket, low scores are not terribly uncommon – although they are not quite so everyday as they used to be. In *Oh! To Be in England* S. P. B. Mais summed it up neatly:

You don't have to sit in the pavilion and watch the slow compilation of centuries. If a side gets thirty runs all told it will probably win.

Village cricket will put you in your place; the element of chance looms so large that you will quickly cease to take your batting or bowling seriously.

Village cricket means that you will lose your contempt for the vicar, and no longer regard the postmaster as a dangerous revolutionary; it is a levelling game.

With all your accoutrements of 'I.Z.' cap, MCC blazer, perfectly creased flannels, well fitting gloves and immaculate pads, you are just as likely to fail to score as the ploughboy who goes in clad in khaki shirt, corduroys, one pad (on the wrong leg), no gloves, using his bat as a scythe.

But, by way of encouragement, Mais adds:

It is quite likely that you will never be found out. One lucky six and you will be famous. Two sixes and your opinion on any subject will be respected. Three and you will be elected MP for the district if you care to stand.

In fact, of course, in modern village cricket you really need to score the best part of 200 before you can relax confidently – although even then you may lose. At the level at which I play, anything in three figures is regarded as a pretty healthy total; in fact, the West Country Publishers have never topped the 200 mark. I have somewhere a pleasing photograph of the scoreboard the day we were all out for 199, the last man out being myself, with a score of approximately 0, and my fellow batsman in the late 90s.

As I say, though, in times gone past the scores in low-level cricket do seem to have been generally quite a lot lower, for some reason which I am not scholar enough to know (probably rotten pitches). To get a typical example of what I mean, I dug through the *Annals of the Teignbridge Cricket Club* and found a record of a three-innings match played between the members in a single day in 1824. True, it was a seven-a-side match, but nevertheless the scores do seem pretty low (especially since, in seven-a-side games, the shortage of batsmen is generally compensated for by the similar shortage of fielders, and, in this case, since many of the players were ex-Eton cricketers). Here is the scorecard:

Match between Members, June 3rd, 1824.

	1st Innings.		2nd Innings		3rd Innings.	
Garrow	c J. Russell	11	c Johnson	4	c J. Russell.	0
Taylor	b J. Russell	3	run out	17	b Johnson.	0
W. Russell	b Johnson.	2	c Wrey	1	run out.	4
Lyon	not out	2	c Wrey	0	run out.	0
Dunn		0	not out	10	b Russell.	0
T. L. Kitson.		0	run out	2	not out.	0
G. Templer.		0	run out	17	b Johnson.	12
Byes		2		2		2
		20		53		18

	1st Innings.		2nd Innings.		3rd Innings.	
Johnson.	c Garrow	11	b Taylor	7	not out.	14
J. Russell	b Taylor	4	caught	5	c Garrow.	0
J. Templer	not out	8	b Garrow	5	b Garrow.	4
J. Wrey	b Garrow	3	caught	0		0
Sir J. Louis.	b Garrow	1	not out	6		0
W. Kitson.		0	run out	1	not out.	0
Acland		0	c J. Russell	3	b Templer.	5
Byes		2		1		12
		29		28		35

Won by three wickets.

Of course, more recent games also have plenty of low scores. In 1979, in a Yorkshire village match between Cawood and Dringhouses, one side was all out for a mere 2 runs. Interestingly, the first ball of the new innings went for 4 byes, and so the winners took the match without having had to actually hit the ball. This was not the first time the feat had been accomplished, however: in 1952 the Surrey team of Bookham succeeded in dismissing a team called the Electrical Trades Commercial Travellers' CC for a grand total of zero, again winning off the first ball of the innings thanks to 4 byes.

Other low scores proliferate. Hawick was dismissed by St Boswells in 1928 for a mere 5. Also in Scotland, a team from the county of Ross was bowled out at Elgin in 1964 for a total of 0 in only 4 overs. The lowest score in any match in which I've played was 15 in a single innings – in fact, it gave me the unique thrill of being able to declare to my wife proudly, on my return home, that I'd been the top scorer for our team in *both* innings: her amazement and hero-worship were substantially reduced when I explained to her that this meant that I'd scored 6 out of 15 in the first innings and 15 out of 31 in the second. Still, if I conveniently forget the precise statistics, I'll have something to tell my grandchildren.

In another match in which I played, the score for one team was almost equally low – but this time it was the opposition who suffered the ignominy. I was playing at the time for the Dartmoor town of Ashburton. We batted first and scored a little over a hundred – enough to make it worth our bowlers' while to try to pull out that little bit extra. They did this to such effect that the opposition (whose name I dare not reveal) were all out for 18. A satisfying victory for Ashburton – except for the fact that the match was all over by half-past four, and the pubs didn't open 'til five-thirty. It was therefore decided between the captains that, in the usual way, there should be a ten-over knockabout to fill in time: in typical fashion, there were special rules, such as nobody being allowed to bowl more than one over.

Things were timed perfectly, and the knockabout ended at 17.25: since it was a five-minute journey to the nearest pub, everybody was perfectly happy. That is, until half-way through the second pint, when the Ashburton team were enraged to hear the enemy skipper say, quite coolly and seriously to the drinkers at large, 'Well, since we won the second match, that makes it one-all.'

But low-scoring matches are not confined to the depths of cricket. In March 1955 New Zealand, facing England, managed to achieve the lowest Test innings total of all time – 26 – their top scorer being Bert Sutcliffe (*not* Herbert Sutcliffe) with a dashing 11. Just before we laugh at the Kiwis, we should remember that other national sides have failed almost equally miserably at Test level. Without going into the statistics of shame too deeply, Australia once scored 36 against England, South Africa 30 against the same opponents, England 45 against Australia, and so on, and on. The lowest innings in a county match was produced by Northamptonshire against Gloucestershire in 1907: the Northants lads scrambled 12. In fact, for the best part of 50 years after their admission to first-class cricket, Northamptonshire went through what can be most tactfully described as a 'bad patch': between 1930 and 1948 the side never appeared higher than second bottom in the county championship, and during that period they once achieved a run of five years during which they stayed right at the bottom, between 1934 and 1938.

Possibly the worst slaughtering of all time came in 1898, when Melbourne University clocked up 1094 against Essendon. The Essendon reply was 76 all out. However, the scores in one village cricket match come close to this. It happened in 1882, when the Orleans Club played Rickling Green. Rickling Green gathered only 94 in their first innings – by no means an unrespectable score for the village cricket of the time – but Orleans, helped by a second-wicket partnership of 507, surpassed this with astonishing ease. By the time stumps were drawn at 6.30, Trevor had 338, Vernon 250, Partridge 90, and Spiro 50, in a total score of 920.

This compares quite well with the highest first-class innings total of all time, 1107 by Victoria against New South Wales in 1926 (but over three days); the highest innings in a Test match, 903 for seven declared, by England against Australia at the Oval in 1938; and certainly with the highest county innings, 887, made by Yorkshire against Warwickshire in 1896.

Some of the low scores of the last century are made all the more remarkable by the fact that the rules of cricket were applied very much more flexibly then. This seems to have been particularly the case when teams from Britain were touring abroad. The team led by W. G. Grace to Australia in 1873–4 was not atypical.

Despite the fact that he was one of the immortals of cricket, and all the other sycophantic bilge you tend to encounter in cricketing books of the rosy-spectacled variety, Grace was ever keen to make the odd buck out of his game – preferably the odd thousand pounds. He'd shocked the Australians by demanding £1500 (a vast sum in those days) plus expenses as a minimum fee for the trip; and he was eager to pick up further payments as the tour progressed. The crunch came towards the end of the tour, when he insisted on getting £800 to play against a South Australian XXII (throughout the trip the home teams had been playing XXIIs against Grace's XI, in order to even up the odds a bit). While the startled South

Australian Cricket Association was still dithering, the little mining town of Kadina, on the Yorke Peninsula on the other side of Gulf St Vincent from Adelaide, suddenly announced that it was prepared to put up the necessary £800 to play against Grace's team.

That Kadina didn't have a cricket pitch was beside the point: the deal was struck. The English arrived, exhausted after a coach trip of some one hundred miles over the primitive roads from Adelaide, to find that the ground was a gravel-covered one – and so hard that water had to be brought to moisten it before the stumps could be driven in. According to a contemporary report in *The Australasian*,

It was impossible to describe the play for the simple reason there was no play to describe. Many victims wouldn't believe they were out, and it afforded considerable merriment to cognoscenti to hear men appealing when clean bowled. The crudeness of their ideas about cricket was wonderful to behold. One man knocked his stump, very nearly spoiling Bush's [the wicketkeeper's] beauty for ever, and then wanted to know if he was out. 'Slightly,' said Bush, but the umpire thought not . . .

Despite such difficulties in understanding the rules of the game, the Kadina miners managed to knock up a total of 42 in the first innings (extras top-scoring with 8). That this was not too bad a total on this barbaric pitch is indicated by the fact that Grace's XI were able to score only 64 in reply. But the second innings of the Kadina XXII must go down in the annals of sport as one of the most disastrous of all time, the English bowler McIntyre taking 7 for 1 and his colleague Lillywhite being comparatively expensive, with 12 for 7. Here is the scorecard:

Perryman caught Boult bowled Lillywhite	2
G. Andrews stumped Bush bowled Lillywhite	2
F. King bowled Lillywhite	0
T Ey bowled Lillywhite	0
J. Bails bowled Lillywhite	0
C. Morton caught Oscroft bowled Lillywhite	0
J. E. Gooden caught Southerton bowled Lillywhite	1
S. Morcom caught & bowled McIntyre	0
E. Andrew caught Bush bowled Lillywhite	1
Rough bowled McIntyre	0
B. Rosman bowled McIntyre	1
J. Ey lbw bowled McIntyre	0
J. Nicholls lbw bowled Lillywhite	0
T. W. Wills bowled Lillywhite	0
J. Upton stumped Bush bowled Lillywhite	0
J. Chittleborough bowled McIntyre	1
H. Arthur bowled McIntyre	0
J. Pinnick *not out*	0
Jewlett bowled McIntyre	0
Paqualin run out	0
S. Nottle bowled Lillywhite	0
Extras	5
TOTAL	**13**

My sympathies have always been for poor old J. Pinnick, stranded there on nought not out: I can imagine him digging himself in, steeling himself to lead a late-order recovery, and then finding that none of his partners at the other end could stay with him long enough.

Although it is actually quite difficult for a XXII to have an innings total as low as 13 (of which only 8 came off the bat), this is by no means the most ignominious score on record among the touring matches. While numerically their feat has been more than equalled, the trophy for utmost shame must go to a Beechwood (Victoria) XI which played during a tour of Australia by H. H. Stephenson and party in the years 1861–2.

Initially this had been planned as a match like any other on the tour: Stephenson's XI versus the Beechwood XXII. However, the match finished rather more speedily than had been expected – the Poms got 264 and then dismissed the Aussies for 20 and 56. In order to fill in some time, therefore, it was proposed that the all-rounder George Griffith take on Beechwood's first XI single-handed. Griffith batted second, and won the match off the first ball he received, which he smote for 2. Beechwood, alas, had notched up only a single run – a bye.

In these terms, then, our opposition's score of 27 seems to be one they can be reasonably proud of. I stand eagerly on the boundary, eyes straining to discern something of the action through the fog. The sound of leather glancing nervously off willow mingles with the fielders' oaths and the batsmen's cries of 'No – no – stay – wait – no – *yes* – COME ON.' This all sounds very hopeful, until we spectators see a white shape approaching us; it proves to be a tight-lipped, ashen Geoff.

'What happened?' I ask. There always has to be some clown who asks a silly question.

'Bloody no-ball,' he says, and refuses to elaborate, beyond applying various further and more extraordinary adjectives to the no-ball. Our scorer, knowing when to keep his head down, has, I later discover, solemnly inscribed in the book 'no-ball – 0' opposite Geoff's name.

It is time for Neil to come in. It's a curious thing but, ever since reading A.G. MacDonell's classic description of a village cricket match in *England, Their England* (1933), I've noticed that every team of village standard or below has a 'village blacksmith'. The player concerned need not in fact *be* a blacksmith – indeed, nowadays, he's almost certainly not – but he has the build, approach and philosophy of life of one. Either he's a demon fast bowler of devastating inaccuracy or a batsman of such brute power that, on the occasions he makes contact with the ball, it soars over nearby housing estates for a resounding six.

Of course, sixes can go a very long way indeed. There are countless tales of mile-long sixes thanks to the ball landing on a passing goods train, or whatever, but these tales are astonishingly difficult to verify. For myself, I like to think that the six scored by Raymond Williams, a rare US cricket fanatic, was the longest of all time. The ball landed well beyond the boundary, and bounced further, into the road and onto a passing 'bus. It was ejected by the conductor only when the 'bus pulled up at the next set of traffic lights.

Williams's claim is quite possibly justified. According to the *Guinness Book of Records* (1982 edition), the longest measured drive on record was a paltry 175 yards, achieved by Walter Fellows in a practice match for Christ Church, Oxford, in 1856.

Of course, this is only the longest *measured* drive. I well remember watching Somerset play Essex in a one-day match, sitting with some friends on the roof of one of the pavilions at that beautiful pitch, Taunton. One member of our company rather dangerously, considering our precarious position, fell asleep for a while, and, as he snoozed, the Essex all-rounder Keith Pont hit a six so huge that we heard it whizzing through the air as it passed some thirty feet above our heads on its way to cause havoc in the car-park behind us. When our friend eventually woke up we told him of this phenomenal blow through which he had slept . . . and he point-blank refused to believe us. Still, I'm sure that the ball travelled much more than 175 yards on that occasion – and would have gone a good deal further had it not become entangled among the parked cars.

Neil, then, is the 'blacksmith' of our side – a 'blacksmith' of the batting variety. The opposition, who have seen him in action before, move most of their fielders around to the leg-side boundary – we know this, because all of a sudden several white backs appear to remind us that there's a game of cricket in progress. It is all to no avail, though. There is a mighty *wallop!* from the direction of the square, and all of a sudden a small, dark, round object sails over the fielders' heads, over the spectators' heads, and lands up with a smack against the changing-room wall.

Someone fetches the ball and tosses it to a fielder, who in turn tosses it in the approximate direction of the bowler. Play is held up for a few moments while the close fielders try to find it; and then the whole process is repeated, only this time Neil doesn't quite get his timing right, so that the ball takes one bounce before crashing against the wall. Unfortunately, that bounce happens to be on the dog-turd one of us squashed while we were practising our bowling, so that there is an acute shortage of volunteers to go and fetch it. Finally Jonathan does so, wiping it off fastidiously on the damp, cloying grass before throwing it in.

By this time the spectators have unanimously decided to move some twenty or thirty yards around the boundary – on the basis that Neil might drop one a bit short, next time. However, there is suddenly a crackling of stumps, a whizzing zing of bails, and a cry of triumph from the centre: Neil's gone, and it's the end of the first over.

He strolls back to the boundary looking both rueful (it was only a couple of minutes ago that he left us) and proud (thanks to him, we're already almost half-way there). From the top of his left pad he pulls out a box of matches, from the top of his right a packet of Number 6: he's able to use this unorthodox mode of carrying his cigarettes around because his innings never involve very much by way of yer actual running between the stumps. In games where he succeeds in getting the ball lost for a while, he's able to light up while waiting patiently at the wicket.

Smoking and 'blacksmiths' seem to go together. The late Jacky Gillott, an ardent cricketer all her life, had to be satisfied with the role of scorer – she was *only* a woman, you see. In one needle-match the side she 'represented' fielded first, and took three wickets in no time at all. The joy was suppressed, though, when the opposition's 'blacksmith' strode purposefully to the crease. The fielders dropped back to the boundary as the bowler – a slow one – strolled in.

The 'blacksmith' did his best to hit the ball into the next county. Indeed, the release of pent-up rotational energy was so great that he spun round in a complete circle and landed on his bottom. The effect was even more dramatic than anticipated for, a keen smoker, he'd gone to the crease carrying a box of Swan Vestas in his back pocket. As he hopped, skipped and yelled, fielders and umpires combined their efforts to beat out the licking flames . . .

With Neil out, it's about time I got padded up – Patrick is already on his way to the wicket. The chances are – damn it – that he'll win the match single-handed. He's easily our best batsman as well as being a useful leg-spinner – in fact, he's the only bowler ever to have injured me: it was embarrassing to have to confess to people over the subsequent weeks that the ugly patch of scar tissue covering much of my upper face was the result of a blow inflicted by a slow leg-break in the nets.

Pads on, I begin to feel something of a nerk. From the sounds wafting across the invisible ground, things are going well for us out there. It seems as if all my efforts in putting on gloves, pads and box and practising a few forward-defensive slogs has been devoted to allowing me the simple pleasure of taking the whole bloody lot off again. And I'm sure that was a contemptuous, mocking glance that one of the 'spectators' just threw at me . . .

Think of it: I haven't bowled, I haven't fielded, and it looks as though I won't be doing any batting. Moreover, I haven't even seen the match . . . and at home there's a great pile of work itching to be done. 'To think!' as a girlfriend of mine once remarked, 'I could have been watching *The Avengers*.' I begin to think of all the other, more pleasurable, ways in which I could have spent this evening rather than standing around in the cold, getting damper and damper. If I were actually *doing* something it would be easier to banish those tantalizing thoughts from my mind.

Professor Sir Bernard Lovell has written of perhaps the ultimate case of cricket taking over the higher functions of the brain. On 12 September 1959, a bright Saturday, he was due to captain his local XI against that of a nearby village. Naturally, his thoughts were almost entirely concentrated upon beating the opposition as thoroughly as possible (as always between neighbouring teams, the rivalry was intense) and preserving his team's unbeaten record for the season; however, he did relax his concentration long enough to call in on Jodrell Bank to make sure nothing much was happening.

Just as he was leaving home for the game, though, a couple of pertinent 'phone calls came through: the Russians were claiming that they had launched a rocket which would crash-land on the Moon the following evening. Sir Bernard was frankly sceptical: Jodrell Bank had been unable to detect the previous Russian attempt to reach the Moon, with Lunik I, early in 1959. This was probably just another example of Red bravura. Still, they were being oddly precise about the predicted impact-time . . .

No matter: there was a cricket match to play. His side batted first, and he put himself low down in the order. The higher-order batsmen added runs easily and quite quickly – and then one of them hit a six which almost shattered the glass of the local 'phonebox. This dragged Lovell's mind unwillingly back to the new Russian probe, Lunik II. Arming himself with enough change, he 'phoned Jodrell Bank (no sign of the rocket, he was told) and his colleague John Davies (they agreed to meet later at the radiotelescope just in case there was something in the Russian claim). And then it was back to the cricket – or, rather, to the cricketing tea.

Immediately after tea the opposition went in to bat. They had a good batting side, including a couple of 'blacksmiths' – one of whom actually *was* a blacksmith. If Lovell's team was to win, he would have to use a considerable deal of guile, making the most of his bowling attack. Two or three overs from himself, and the same from the other fastish bowler, then bring on the leg-spinner . . .

Only the blacksmith to worry about now. I wonder where that rocket is. Let me see – must have been launched about 1 P.M. our time, escape velocity 11km per sec. – oh! why do I always remember rocket velocities in metric and the distance to the Moon in miles? Six o'clock, 50 for 2, and they don't like it, they're beginning to block. Must shift this pair. Let me see, 11km per second – that would be about 7 miles per second, 400-odd miles per minute – yes, that's right, about 25,000 miles per hour. Must already have travelled 100,000 miles and we haven't got these chaps out yet. Ah, there goes his leg-stump thank heavens, it's the other opener, never did like bowling or fielding to left-handers. Still, we don't know the orbit and can't think that one out now. In any case it can't be as far from Earth as that, so we ought to have ample signal strength if only we could find it. Here comes their number five: the blacksmith. Must concentrate on the cricket. He could double the score in the next half-hour if we're not careful . . .

And so it went on. The astonishing thing is that Lovell was able to captain his side to victory while simultaneously performing orbital calculations in his head. Most fellow-denizens of the depths of cricket would, of course, have been forced to put such things from their minds.

Sir Bernard escaped from the post-match carousings at the earliest possible opportunity and drove quickly to Jodrell Bank. There he found a crowd of American space scientists as well as journalists from various countries, all complaining bitterly because throughout the entire afternoon the only response to any of their questions had been that nothing could be done until Lovell appeared, and he was at the moment playing cricket. He kept his air nonchalant until he unlocked the door to the room containing the telex machine: there, spewing out over the floor, was precise information as to the launch-time, orbital configuration, radio-transmitter frequencies, velocity . . .

The following evening, as I've no doubt you can well remember, Lunik II became the first space-probe to cross all those lonely miles to reach the Moon.

There is a sudden burst of applause which limps through the mists from the direction of the square. White shapes – lots of them – begin to emerge unsteadily from the overall obscurity: the match is clearly over. Grumpily, I strip off my pads and gloves as unobtrusively as possible and throw them into the bag. As I haven't really done anything except walk a couple of hundred yards and jump up and down a few times since putting on my whites, I might as well not bother changing; the local pub must be accustomed to serving eager drinkers dressed all in white. The other players divide into two quite distinct classes: those whose whites are, like mine, absolutely pristine; and those who by some fluke have actually been able to do some fielding – they're decorated with broad, black and green, macho smirches of mud and grass, as if Van Gogh and Jackson Pollock had both attacked the same canvas in rapid succession.

Afterwards, in the pub, I try to decide within myself which is the worst: the pub itself or the beer it serves. I still haven't made up my mind when somebody says to me, inevitably, 'Ah, cricket. It's a funny old game, isn't it?'

'Bloody funny,' I mutter into my mugful of extremely expensive slops, 'especially when you play.'

3
THE WIMPOLE MATCH
9th June, 1983

'What'll you have to drink?' I ask Jonathan. It is a beautiful summer's evening – the type of evening that cricket was invented for – and we are in the bar of a peculiarly undistinguished pub. None of your thatched roof and blackened oak beams here. Instead there are several fruit machines that intermittently interrupt all conversation by producing a noise like a computer farting, posters telling us to buy Harvey Wallbangers, groups of young trendies bent on showing the world that they are having a Hell of a Good Time, tastefully patterned carpets that won't show beer splatters, ash droppings or vomit stains, and nice bright lights so that the customers won't be distracted by the early-evening sunlight pouring in through the plate-glass windows.

'I'll have a half of lager,' he says after some thought.

'Nance,' I say automatically, but I order it for him along with a pint of fizzy bitter for myself. The drinks arrive, and I repeat: 'Nance' – but this time with feeling. The lager has been served up in the most curvaceously feminine glass ever designed by Man. Jonathan seizes it with a blush and a stammer and virtually scampers to a table hidden from the rest of the bar by one of the louring fruit machines.

I join him more sedately.

He has his revenge. 'You do realize we've only got a few minutes before we have to go to the ground,' he says. 'You'd better drink that pint up fast.'

I look at it. There is no way that anyone is going to complain to the publican that his beer is flat: it looks like a shandy that has been mixed in a cocktail shaker. If I down it in five minutes – which I will, because being a Scot I don't like to see anything wasted – I am going to register on the Richter scale for most of the evening. 'At least it's in a decent glass,' I mutter weakly.

Somehow the conversation turns to the origins of figures of speech – which are understood by everybody but have no literal meaning. Who invents them, and how do they ever come to be invented in the first place?

'Take another example,' says Jonathan after a while. '"Like a bat out of hell". Bats don't live in hell – and, if they did, there's no reason to believe they'd exit any faster than anyone else. I mean, if you think about it, bats don't actually fly very quickly – they tend to sort of swoop and swirl.'

'It must be a corruption of some other saying,' I remark. 'You know, originally it meant something, but over the centuries it was distorted by constant repetition until it became "like a bat out of hell". My guess is that it was born as a cricketing expression.'

'That seems to make sense,' says Jonathan, his eyes suddenly taking on a faraway look. I can tell that – oh, God – a piece of lunacy is on its way. 'The old legends have it all wrong,' he says abruptly. 'The man wasn't an archer at all. He batted at number four for Switzerland for many years. Hence the expression, "like the bat of William Tell".'

Disgustedly, I finish my beer in silence, break that silence with a belch, and stand up. 'We'd better go and play some cricket,' I say.

The ground at Wimpole is one of the prettiest I've ever seen. It is surrounded on all sides by trees – one of which, a huge one, actually stands inside the boundary. The local rule is that if you hit the tree it's a four, or a six if the ball doesn't touch the ground en route. Adrian

Male, a slow off-spinner, has told me that he has at least once had good reason to be grateful to that tree while bowling for Wimpole. His first ball of the game was cheerfully dispatched into its topmost branches by the opposing batsman, but the umpire promptly declared that it had been a null-ball – not a no-ball – because, through oversight, there had been no umpire at square leg. He instructed the scorers to treat the ball as if it had never been bowled. The batsman was not pleased.

Adrian was, though. Making as little fuss as possible, he planted several fielders around the tree, and then bowled an identical ball. Sure enough, the frustrated batsman tried to respond to it with an identical shot, and was elegantly caught by one of the fielders.

The umpire's decision concerning the null-ball was, of course, correct – but at our level of cricket you cannot usually expect the umpires to show such a grasp of the game's rules. The problem is exacerbated by the fact that every team's 'superstars' – the crack opening batsmen and the demon bowlers – show little inclination to put in a stint of umpiring. The task is instead generally allocated to those whose number in the batting order is rarely in single figures – and who, for that reason, are likely to be less familiar with the subtleties of the rules than are their more illustrious team-mates. In the team for which I play, this means that Rudolph and I are generally the first ones to put on the white coats, to act as judges over the batting of our fellows – which would be all very well except that I am a bowler by instinct (on one occasion I found myself going up with a cry of 'howzatt!' for someone else's caught-behind) and Rudolph is one of those courageous people who's never afraid of taking a tough or unpopular decision: if the ball hits the batsman on the pads, that's almost certainly it, wherever he's standing. But at least we do our best to be impartial.

Some umpires, by contrast, are definitely hostile – either to batsmen in general or to bowlers in general. It is not always easy to work out why this should be so – but Colin Cracknell, of Heston Cricket Club, has told me of one instance in which it was only too obvious what had happened. He was playing against Exmouth while on a tour of Devon. One member of the team travelled to the match alone, in a red sports car. Perhaps it was the redness of the sports car that did it, but friend Andrew had a brush with the police on the way, and was further held up on arrival by a bolshie car-park attendant. His temper was already short when he finally reached the pitch, late, and then he received a dressing-down from his skipper . . . He was sentenced to several overs' umpiring duty.

Cracknell and his team-mate Wilson had opened the batting, and were sailing along merrily enough: 35 for no wicket. The Exmouth ground is rather a lovely one, only a few dozen yards from the sea, and many batsmen find it conducive to scoring a few runs. The pair looked set for a good opening partnership.

The Exmouth skipper brought on a leg-spinner. Leg-spinners at the very highest levels can be devastating attack bowlers, but at the more lowly levels they tend at best to be erratic and, more often, good friends to batsmen. (All leg-spinners reading these words are, of course, exceptions to this general rule.) Cracknell and Wilson felt with some justification that, if only they kept their heads – which is not always easy to do against a leg-spinner – there were plenty of runs to be had. They licked their lips.

But then Andrew arrived in his white coat, still muttering under his breath, and Wilson was given out lbw off the very next ball.

Colin Cracknell felt that he had to protest – modestly –

to the umpire. 'Er, surely that ball pitched outside the leg stump. And, er, Andrew, to cap it all the bowler coughed.'

The sole response was a red-eyed glare, and a few taut words: 'He was out – and I'm going to get you in a minute, too.' And he did.

Cracknell, who is these days President of Heston Cricket Club, has also passed on to me one of the most sadistic tales of umpiring I've come across. Not long after the Second World War he was playing for an Old Boys' XI against a local team which enjoyed the services of an extremely fast, dangerous bowler. As so often happens, the Old Boys' XI were one short, and so they persuaded the wing half of the corresponding Old Boys' soccer team to turn out for them. This he did with some reluctance. While he was something of a star at football he had never been much of a cricketer – and, in particular, he hated fast bowling.

The demon paceman had just returned to the attack when the footballer, a stocky man, came to the wicket. The score was a not very respectable 80 for 8. As the first delivery came scorching down, the batsman instinctively ducked – straight into the path of the ball, which struck him, according to Cracknell, 'a terrible blow on the left ear'. He collapsed onto the turf.

As he was being carried off a few minutes later, still in great pain and suffering the effects of concussion, he was no doubt greatly cheered to hear the umpire bellow after him: 'And don't bring him back – he was lbw.'

Robert Holles, in his delightful *The Guide to Real Village Cricket* (1983), tells the tale of a rather similar umpiring decision. One of the members of the side which had batted first had committed the cardinal discourtesy of scoring a century, and now – horror of horrors – was being brought on to bowl, too. Almost immediately he sent up a stentorian lbw appeal, to which the umpire made a politely 'stertorian' response. A couple of overs later, the bowler tried the unsportsmanlike trick of running out the backing-up batsman without having given him any prior warning. Once again he appealed – and this time in such a way as to make his earlier histrionics seem like little more than a shy cough.

But again the umpire turned down the appeal, saying: '. . . 'ow would you like it if I gave *you* out, just because some silly bugger whipped the bails off when 'e was supposed to be bowlin'?'

The bowler, clearly a glutton for punishment, continued to . . . violently disagree.

After a while the umpire added quietly: 'Anyway, it was a no-ball, now I come to think about it.'

But there are plenty of other ways in which umpires can stamp their personalities upon games aside from biased decisions, hostility to bowlers or batsmen, or just plain incompetence. Roy Hattersley has written of the one time he played at the legendary Bramall Lane – for Wadsley Church Youth Club against Sheffield United Under Sixteens. The opposition bowlers were of such a terrifying pace that young Roy was demoted from opening to number three – a tactical decision that made very little difference, in the event, because the first wicket went down almost immediately. At last his dreams – or his nightmares? – were coming true:

I asked, as always, for 'middle and leg'. No doubt as a help to my cricket education the umpire replied 'two leg' in mild reproof and correction. And that was only the beginning of his unintentional intimidation. He was an elderly member of the Bramall Lane staff who had been relegated to supervision of the young. As part of his coaching duties he instructed the bowlers in the setting of fields. There is something particularly unnerving in preparing to take strike and suddenly noticing that the *umpire* is reinforcing the slips.

In fact, there is one thing much more unnerving than that, and it is to watch the reactions of one amateur umpire notorious for his dubious decisions when he has just been given out as a result of someone else's dubious decision. Rudolph, from our team, was once heard to remark by anyone within a five-mile radius, as he hurled his bat vindictively at the pavilion wall: 'I was *not* caught behind. I know I missed the ball. I know better than anyone else in this club what it's like to miss the ball. I have vast experience of missing the ball. I missed it completely . . .'

A little after six o'clock, the scheduled kick-off time, something begins to dawn on us all. There are eleven of us here, complete with our kit, but as yet no member of the opposition has turned up. They are definitely a little late. Perhaps, we snarl at the fixtures secretary, he got the time wrong? Maybe it was supposed to be a six-thirty start? I am certain that I hear Jonathan mutter: 'I would have had time for another half of lager.' But maybe not, maybe not.

The yobs among us – of whom there are about nine, including myself – have dug into the kit bag to get out a few balls and a bat, and are putting in some much-needed fielding practice. This consists of one's erstwhile friends bowling at one's unprotected legs with bone-shattering viciousness, while, in return, one tries to hit the ball with such ferocity that they have to run a long way to retrieve it. An alternative technique is to smite it straight back at them with colossal force, and then laugh at them as they drop the catch and swear at their bruised hands. Since I can bowl rather more dangerously and bat only rather more milksoppishly than most, my body becomes a prime target when it is my turn for a spell of batting. I develop the art of the extremely late, extremely fine cut – which involves my attempting to wallop the ball as hard as possible but mistiming the shot completely so that the ball snicks off the edge of the bat to speed into the shrubbery behind the pavilion. The hapless bowler then has to run all the way round to fetch it.

There is something of a dream-like quality about the whole situation. There are no sounds at all from the nearby village; hardly a vehicle roars along the lane beside the pitch. There is very little wind, so only occasionally do the trees sigh out across the field. The sunlight is beginning to take on a slightly orange tinge. Here we are, the eleven of us, for all the world like the groups of people one sees in grotty adventure movies who have found themselves somehow transported to the land beyond the vortex of the Bermuda Triangle – as if we were uncertain how or why we had come to this place. I muse idly along these lines, with the result that I get hit on the ankle. To reduce still further my self-image from that of poet to that of village idiot, as I limp off cursing weakly the fly on my trousers abruptly disintegrates.

Boxes have, of course, been the item of cricketing garb most subject to cheap jokes and hoary legends – the mothers-in-law of cricketing tales, as it were – but I've always felt that in fact the garment whose sudden failure can cause the greatest loss of dignity is the humble pair of white trousers. Sometimes, to be fair, they can be an additional weapon in the cricketer's armoury. In a 1959 match in New Zealand, for example, the batsman hit the ball straight at gully, who completely misjudged the potential catch. However, it hit his foot and, by chance, ran up his trouser-leg. When he had finally worked it out again he held it up in triumph and appealed for the catch. Appeal granted.

More usually, though, cricketing trousers are possessed of a sadistic maliciousness which provokes them to plunge

even the most dignified of players from the pillar of
solemnity into the pit of ridicule. This is especially true if
they are *my* trousers: I was once warned by an umpire
for attempting to distract the batsman, because my flies
were cheerfully unzipping themselves each time I ran in
to bowl. I swore that day never to wear bright scarlet
underpants again.

Very often trousers' rebelliousness springs from the
fact that they are borrowed: let's face it, if *you* were a
pair of trousers, would you like to be lent to a sweaty
stranger? Bill Pullen has told me of a Gotherington game
in which he played in 1971, when he was forced to borrow
a pair of flannels from 'our rather portly captain. They
had no belt loops, so I put a thin, tight belt around them
and hoped for the best. During the stand, while at the
bowler's end, I suddenly felt them slipping at the back.'
He was left standing with his trousers round his ankles
while the rest of the players loudly admired his multi-
coloured pants.

Ronnie Locke suffered from the descending-trouser
syndrome in rather a different way when playing for
Cheadle Hulme against Alderley Edge in the 1984 George
Newton Trophy Final:

Cheadle Hulme had batted first and scored 234–5 in their 40
overs. Alderley Edge were going well at 80–3 off 11 overs,
when the Cheadle Hulme captain, Dave Hancock (ex Stafford-
shire and Minor Counties), was hit in the face whilst fielding at
mid off, and had to leave the field. Not having an official 12th
man, we asked one of our second-XI players, Ian Brown, who
was spectating, to put on Hancock's kit and field for us.

The game continued whilst Ian got changed. When he
appeared on the pavilion steps suitably attired, I was about to
start an over of off-spin. As the pavilion was on the square-leg
boundary, and I required a deep square leg, it was sensible to
ask him to field in front of the packed pavilion.

The first ball of the over was swept by the batsman high in

the direction of substitute Brown. He, a very good boundary
fielder, realizing he had about eight yards to make round the
boundary to get under the ball, set off in the appropriate
direction. He never made it. He was still three yards short
when his borrowed flannels fell down. He grasped at them,
catching them as they reached mid-thigh, and the ball crossed
the boundary first bounce.

Brown's embarrassment was one stage more acute than if
he had been wearing brightly coloured underpants.

All ended happily, however. The fielder borrowed a
belt, and when the batsman attempted an identical shot
off the next ball Brown took a superb catch – starting a
batting collapse by Alderley Edge, who were all out for
137.

Batting collapses were, of course, rather easier to
contain in the days when weaker teams might field more
players than their stronger opponents: 22 against 11 was
not uncommon. In the year 1870, for example, Lords &
Commons Cricket fielded 24 men against their regular
rivals, I Zingari, who played with only 12. In fact, it was
the custom in the matches between the two clubs for
Lords & Commons Cricket to bolster their strength
not only with extra players but also with one or two
professionals as well as, on occasions when sudden
debates in the House caused problems, members of the
parliamentary staff, the police of 'A' Division, and so on.
No doubt it was purely a matter of coincidence that these
substitutes were on the whole rather younger and fitter
than those they replaced.

The tradition of Lords & Commons Cricket goes back
a long way. The club was founded in about 1845, which
makes it older than all the first-class clubs with the
possible exceptions of Sussex and Northamptonshire. In
his rare book, *A History of Lords & Commons Cricket*
(*c*. 1958), Eric Bullus cites a newspaper account of the

club's first recorded match – which was, like so many others, against I Zingari, which itself had not long before been founded. The account is full of leaden nineteenth-century facetiousness, but has its moments of interest.

'My gracious Lord, here in the Parliament
Let us assail the family' etc. etc.

'The Commons haply rise' – (*Henry VI*, part 3) – and Trojan-like, duly impressed with the idea that 'when Greek meets Greek then comes the tug of war,' buried in oblivion the all-absorbing question of the pacific Greek war and left to Baron Gros and those of grosser growth to decide the knotty point 'whence grows this insolence.' Saturday, the 22nd inst., led on by Serjeant-at-Arms, the Lords and Commons did repair to Vincent Square to square cricket accounts with I Zingari. The late division of the previous night having delayed the arrival of a portion of the senatorial Eleven – a motion was brought forward to Lord Burghley and Wisden (who played as a substitute for Lord Ward [a sneaky substitution, that one]) do take their positions at the wicket; which was carried without a division and the remainder of the senators did obtain leave to sit (down) again:

'Consedêre ducês, intentique ora tenebant'

i.e. freely translated:

'The Leaders sat down and being in tent
Put their heads in their hands on their knee bent.'

Lord Burghley proved that the change from bachelor to ben-edick [married man] had made no change in the science of batting, which in both innings proved passing excellent. The fine play of Mr Curteis (MP for Rye) caused many wry faces on the I Z. side. He succeeded in carrying out his bat in spite of the repeated red hot spots from the hands of the artillerymen and of the united efforts of Messrs. Duff, Introbus, Bligh and Mostyn, whose bowling in the first innings was extremely good. In the second innings, the ground, having been newly laid down, was much broken up, thus rendering the bowling anything but an agreeable task, in short an illustration of 'breaking up, no holiday.' [I suspect a word or two has been missed from that sentence: surely it must have been *facing* the bowling which was 'anything but an agreeable task'.] The reappearance of Lord Verulam in flannels and bat in hand, gave great satisfaction to those whose memory carried them to the top of the tennis court at Lord's, o'er which in days gone by he drove a cricket ball; his power of leg-hitting appeared to have retained a corner in his memory. Colonel Lowther, who contributed 17 runs in good style, was, unfortunately, run out after a fine hit to the off. If it takes nine tailors to make a man, Colonel Taylor proved that it takes eleven to mar one; after some fine hitting, he fell a martyr to Mr Mostyn. Lord Darnley scored within one of a score; a good example, implicitly followed by his brother, Mr Bligh, who was opposed to him. Mr Bagge, as long-stop, cannot be passed over without commendation, nor can Mr Ker's boldness in the same position in the I Z. remain unnoticed: the former gentleman was unfortunate in his innings, which terminated somewhat abruptly by his breaking his bail. The innings of I Zingari commenced unfortunately, that leary little man Wisden, having hurried Mr Micklethwaite back to the tent – however, Messrs. Morse and Whitehead were leary in their reciprocal admonition –

'Pray you, let us hit together'

and found 48 runs in a quick 25 minutes. The remaining I Z. presented singular figures – on the score – and fell victims all, with the exception of one run out, to the wily Wisden.

It is hardly surprising that the I Zingari batsmen had some difficulty playing against John Wisden, for he was one of the finest bowlers in the land, representing during his career Sussex, the All-England XI and the United England XI. In a match between North and South in 1850 he took ten wickets in an innings, all clean bowled, and in the following year he took no less than 455 wickets. He was a fast bowler who could make the ball cut in sharply from the off.

Lords & Commons Cricket now played their second innings, and the newspaper correspondent, so garrulous about their first, is ominously brief in his account of it:

Nearly eight o'clock – 'Termination of the innings of both Houses of Parliament.'

Eight o'clock – 'Motion – that the innings of I Z. do take place that day six months. No opposition offered.'
Eight 30 – 'Members rapidly quitting.'
Eight 45 – 'I Z. left sitting. No division expected.'

One gets the impression that any I Zingari innings would have been merely a formality. So far as I can establish, there was no winter fixture played 'that day six months' for the formality to be completed, but there was a return match just one month after that first fixture, and thereafter the sides played each other once or twice a year.

From somewhere there has been born the myth that for many years there was an annual cricket match between the Commons and the Lords, so I was slightly surprised, when I went up to Westminster in late 1984 to talk about the subject with Susan Carter, secretary to Michael Mates MP (current Secretary of Lords & Commons Cricket), to discover that the several references I had found to such matches were canards of one kind or another. In fact, there seem to have been only three Commons *versus* Lords matches, the first of which was only a single-wicket match, between Lord Skelmersdale and T. de Grey MP. Precise references – such as the date of this match – are hard to glean from the scanty records of Lords & Commons Cricket, but it is known that in this single-wicket contest there were two fielders on each side, that wides and no-balls did not count, and that the scores were: Skelmersdale 6 and 12; Grey 3 and 16 not out – Grey therefore winning despite a shaky start. The umpires were drawn one from each House, to ensure impartiality. It all sounds rather like a knockabout on the common: indeed, it's astonishing that the scores weren't far higher, with so few fielders.

Similarly, there are on record only three cricket

matches between the Government and the Opposition, played in 1861, 1862 and 1863. Not much is known about them, except that the Opposition won the first.

Lords & Commons Cricket does not have a proud record of success. In 43 matches played against Westminster School between 1922, when Lords & Commons Cricket was revived, and 1939, the parliamentary team won 15, lost 20 and drew 8; and between 1951 and 1958 their only victory over the school was in 1957. They did, however, sometimes put up a brave effort in this period: it was against Westminster School that Lords & Commons Cricket recorded its only postwar century – 102 not out by William Bromley-Davenport in 1952. Despite his fine effort, they still lost.

Of 16 matches played between Lords & Commons Cricket and the MCC, Lords & Commons won only 2 – but they did manage to record a tie. This was in 1932, when Lords & Commons were chasing a target of 178. Off the last ball of the second-last over Sir Waldron Smithers took a single to level the scores. He then squared up to face the bowling of the great Gubby Allen – who shattered his stumps to matchwood. To celebrate the occasion, the Governor of I Zingari, the Earl of Dartmouth, ceremoniously sent to the Lords & Commons captain, Sir Rowland Blades, a tie of the sartorial kind. This Sir Rowland Blades was, by the way, a leg-spinner, and such a keen bowler that on at least one occasion he bowled before the batsman had taken his guard.

Lords & Commons bowling seems to have had its ups and downs. In 1951 Aidan Crawley MP took the club's only postwar hat-trick, against the Egyptian team of Fares Sarofeem's XI – in fact, he ended up with figures of 6 for 35 in 14 overs, which no bowler would regard as shameful. But at the other end of the scale there is a record (alas, undated) of a match in which Lord Hawke was demonstrating the art of slow bowling. In his first two overs he conceded 28 runs, and the first four balls of his third over were hit for 2, 6, 4 and 6, respectively. At that point the opposition declared. As the Lords & Commons players retreated from the field, Lord Hawke was heard to mutter: 'Pity. Just when I'd got him guessing . . .'

Lords & Commons Cricket is still an active club, playing about a dozen matches a year. There is no regular captain as such, each match being organized by a 'match manager' – or even, on occasion, two match managers. Regular fixtures are still played against the MCC and Westminster School, as well as against St Paul's School and the BBC. An interesting annual fixture is the match against the Dutch Parliament, played in Britain and Holland in alternate years. One gets the impression, though, that there is rather less enthusiasm among the people's representatives than in past decades – or maybe it's simply that in these modern times they feel that there are more important issues to decide than the winner of a cricket match.

In a way they're right, if this is the case. But I have a fantasy that, if all the leading politicians in the country or even in the world were forced to play against each other in a dozen cricket matches a year, political life would consist of far less by way of stupid macho posturing and far more by way of reasoned searching for the best solutions to the various problems facing us all. For example, Willy, who plays for our team, has political views diametrically opposed to my own, yet in the pub after a game we can discuss my superb economic analyses and his political illiteracies in a civilized fashion, buying each other drinks the while. Just as importantly, I will strain every sinew to pick up a catch off his bowling, and he off mine.

It makes you think, doesn't it? Or, come to think of it, it probably shouldn't.

The half-hour chimes out resonantly over the greensward from the distant village church. There is just the slightest hint of haze in the purpling shadows beneath the dappled trees, as somewhere a cow lows mournfully. Upon the grass of the outfield, nigh on a dozen lusty swains in white disport themselves, filling the air with the traditional sound of leather smacking willow. Ah, yes, this is England now that summer's here. This is the England about which the pastoral poets have waxed eulogistically. A tractor chunters by along the lane, a cheery farmer grinning with his stolid Anglo-Saxon face at us. Hark – was that a plover?

On the other hand, where the bloody hell's the opposition?

Bart, our captain today, is beginning to look very worried indeed. 'The trouble is,' he says to somebody, 'I just can't remember the bastard's name. Obviously I didn't bother bringing his 'phone number . . . but if I could remember his effing name I could look him up in the bloody book.'

I sense that, as with me, all romantic images of mellow, merrie Englande have abruptly disappeared from Bart's mind. Unfair though it may be, we are all beginning to cast him in the role of scapegoat. Our appetites have been whetted for cricket – even more so now that most of us have had a knockabout – and some of us have driven quite considerable distances (well, thirty miles or so) to get here. The opposition's fixtures secretary is not in evidence, and anyway it's always so much more *fun* to assume that any cock-up is the fault of the person who's actually here. It must be Bart's fault – it must. He was the member of our team who was supposed to have fixed up this match: he's obviously got the date wrong, or the place wrong, or something.

I was once involved in a match where the opposite happened. The day had not been too good – a bit of rain here and there – and so I, like everyone else in the team, had 'phoned the captain just to make sure the game was going ahead. 'I've just been on the 'phone to their captain,' said ours, 'and he says it's all OK.' Two teams turned up at the pitch to discover that the groundsman, rather than bothering to get in touch with anybody, had simply chalked up a notice saying that the pitch was unfit for play. The player who'd lost overtime pay and driven over fifty miles to get there was among the least amused.

'Can't you 'phone Celia?' I say to Bart. 'Presumably she'd be able to dig out the number.'

'Celia's gone round to visit her sister,' says Bart miserably.

'Why don't we just set up our stumps and have a practice match?' someone suggests. I realize with sudden horror that it's me.

'You can't do that,' says Bart. 'You can't just foul up someone else's pitch.'

'Why not?' says a chorus. 'They're the [astonishingly inventive expletives deleted] who've let us down.'

Bart suddenly claps his forehead. 'I've remembered the bastard's surname!' he cries. 'I'll go and find a telephone box and see what I can do.' With undisguised relief he leaps into his car and is gone. With similarly undisguised relief I leap behind the pavilion for a piddle: now I know why Jonathan stuck to a half of lager.

Curiously enough, piddles can have their effects on games of cricket. Years ago, when we first formed the predecessor of the club for which I now play, we were very conscious of the fact that none of us had played the game for years – in some cases, for well over a decade.

We therefore asked the teachers of a local school if they would put up a side as opposition for our initial match, explaining to them the circumstances: 'Ur, we weren't terribly good to begin with, and after all these years . . .' Their tactless response was to include in their side the opening batsman for one of the major local league teams.

We had heard about this the day of the match, and so we decided that, beforehand, we'd congregate in Newton Abbot's celebrated Cider Bar to have what is euphemistically described as 'net practice' in order to steel ourselves for the forthcoming disaster. By the time we reached the pitch, there was no question that anyone could accuse us of not having had sufficient net practice.

The star batsman – whom I shall call Gladys because that most definitely is not his name – set about my bowling, and that of my opening partner, with a will: our averages very soon began to look like those of Lord Hawke. But then Willy, my old chum and bitter political enemy, fielding on the boundary, played his master-stroke. The cider inside him was beginning to seek release from the confines of his body, and so he spoke urgently to one of the opposition sitting on the boundary line: could he take over just for a couple of minutes while Willy leapt behind a bush? Indeed he could – glad to help.

The next ball I bowled was not so much a bad one as a very bad one. Short, outside the leg stump – you name it. Gladys gave an anticipatory leer, and with a twist of his muscular shoulders hit it far into the middle distance . . . and, as it proved, straight into the waiting hands of the substitute fielder. Gladys was not pleased. I think, although I am not sure, that he kicked his bat several times on the way back to the boundary. Willy emerged from behind his bush with the smug grin of someone who has just taken a vital wicket. The substitute laughed as he threw a matey arm around Gladys' shoulder, only to have it shrugged off furiously. I hopped around like a thing demented, remarking to all and sundry about my sophisticated field-placings.

The fevered conversation on the boundary continued throughout the opposition's innings.

Bowlers can get rid of even the best opposition batsmen in curious ways. In his definitive *This Curious Game of Cricket* (1982) George Mell draws from *The History of Radley College* the strange tale of a fast bowler who got rid of three opposing batsmen with a single delivery. He hit the striker on the thumb, causing such profuse bleeding that the batsman had to retire. At the opposite end, the other batsman fainted, presumably from the sight of so much gore, and had to be helped off the pitch. Finally one of the incoming batsmen sized up the situation and announced resolutely that he had decided to take no further part in the game.

Not always are these debilitating injuries inflicted by fast bowlers, however. A mixture of kindness and cruelty attended one match played by the Irish club Chapelizod. They had reached the final of a Junior Village Cup competition – but there was a snag about their team-selection process for this important match. The club treasurer was a doughty and popular fellow but . . . well, the trouble was that he wasn't much of a cricketer. He turned out whenever he was asked, and nobody ever begrudged him his place in a normal match, but for this one . . . ? What could they do? They didn't want to hurt his feelings by dropping him, but at the same time they wanted to make absolutely sure they won the match.

They waited until they were playing a friendly match a couple of weeks before the crucial final. The treasurer was pressed into doing a stint of umpiring duty and, while standing at square leg, was deftly felled by a hook shot from one of the stars of the Chapelizod batting line-up.

He was still limping on the day of the final, but watched enthusiastically as his side swept to triumph. Some days later he appeared before the local magistrates to be fined for drunken behaviour at the match. Surely a low-level cricketer who deserves every ounce of our admiration.

I am brought back to reality by the return of Bart. He screeches to a halt and leaps out of his car with a jaunty smile of confidence. Oh, good, at last we're going to have a game of cricket, I think. 'No,' says Bart. 'I got in touch with their fixtures secretary all right, and he told me that he'd forgotten all about the game. He's kind of sorry, but there's no way that he can rustle up a side even for a ten-over knockabout – half his lot aren't on the 'phone.'

The species – even the genus – of the fixtures secretary's parentage is brought into question by a chorus of discordant voices. The general level of stark hatred casts my mind back to my fantasy about cricket being a great political balm. I'm not suggesting that re-establishing cricketing links with South Africa would do anything to ameliorate that nation's foul racism – far from it: welcoming South Africa in from the cold would be regarded as a triumph for the apartheid regime. But it still strikes me that if, say, Pik Botha were persuaded to face a few overs from, say, Michael Holding or Imran Khan or Kapil Dev, and then to share a meal or a drink with them afterwards, he'd suddenly get a whole new perspective on the idiotic notion of white supremacy. Certainly the principle works in this country: down here in the West most people are generally less cosmopolitan than their London counterparts, because there are very few blacks, yellows or whatever that live here. Nevertheless, there is hardly any racial prejudice – and to a great extent this is probably due to the fact that the local heroes in this part of the world include such figures as Viv Richards, Joel Garner and Hallam Moseley; Sunil Gavaskar, too, was a local hero for a while.

We find support for this general political idea in an essay by George Mikes which appears in Allen Synge's enjoyable anthology *Strangers' Gallery* (1974). Mikes is, of course, the Hungarian whose observations of the English are more perceptive than those of any Englishman. In the essay he tells how he – and cricket – did their bit to ease British-Israeli tensions in the early years after Israel's establishment. He was in Israel doing some research for a book, and was in continual touch with the British Embassy. British relations with the *kibbutzniks* were not good. The *kibbutzniks* distrusted the British, for obvious reasons, even though many of the *kibbutzniks* themselves came from Britain. For their part, the British were none too keen on the *kibbutzniks* – 'partly because they found them unlikeable,' says Mikes, 'and partly because they were in love with the Arabs.'

The British diplomats were not happy – and eventually one of them told Mikes that life would be much more bearable if only they could have the occasional game of cricket. Mikes asked them why on earth they didn't just have one, and was patronizingly told that he, a mere foreigner, didn't understand that to play cricket you need two teams of eleven players each: there simply weren't enough people in the embassy.

A couple of weeks later Mikes, by chance, had a very similar conversation with a *kibbutznik*. The members of this particular kibbutz came largely from Manchester and, while they loved their new-found home, realized that something very important was missing: cricket. The trouble was that there were not enough of them to muster two teams.

Mikes did the obvious: he put the two sets of people in touch. Of course, neither really *wanted* to play the other, but . . . well, when you're on the cricket pitch trifles such as deep, inalienable hatred tend to be ignored. As Mikes himself put it: 'I should like to believe that my initiative contributed not only to the personal happiness of a few cricketing enthusiasts but helped to lay the foundations of a stronger and firmer British-Israeli understanding.' It almost certainly did.

All of a sudden, as we sit in the pub, someone is shouting: 'Well, I think it's a bit bloody much if the opposition fail to turn up. We won't play those [even more inventive expletives deleted] again.'

'Until next year,' says someone.

I cast my mind back to the time I came to another match where the opposition failed to appear. On that occasion the captain – whose name I forget – not only succeeded in contacting the fixtures secretary but also persuaded him to rustle up a scratch team. The day was freezing, and the ground treacherous underfoot. Not long after we'd started, it began to rain, but, since we'd all made the effort to be there, we played on. I was not called upon to bowl, for some reason (probably stark ineptitude), and was put in to bat at number 11, where I made a glamorous nought not out, without facing a ball.

All in all, I conclude, staring into my really quite reasonable pint, I'm glad the Wimpole match turned out the way it did . . .

Part Two
1984

4
THE ABBOTSKERSWELL MATCH
20th May, 1984

The nets have been good for me this year. We've had about six or seven sessions of them, all but one characterized by the lack of enthusiasm on the part of the club members. With the exception of that one occasion, the only people at the net practices have been Bart, Jonathan and myself. While this has been, perhaps, a bad thing for the club, it has certainly been a good thing for the three of us. Both Bart and I are bowling much faster and more accurately than either of us can remember having done for some years; Jonathan has suddenly discovered how to bowl a vicious in-swinger (or, at least, he hasn't really discovered *how* to: it's just that, for the first time in his life, he's able to regularly do so); and all three of us are batting with great confidence. Even I have found out how to play a devastatingly forceful cut – the first known stroke I've ever developed which does not hurtle the ball at catching height amongst the on-side fielders.

At one of our practice sessions – on a beautifully hot, sunny, West Country Sunday – the script was definitely written by Brian Clemens, on holiday from *The Avengers*. Bart snicked a ball which I had sent down to him, and it went high up behind him, through a hole at the back of the net, and over an imposing brick wall. Since cricket balls don't come two a penny, and especially since this was a newish one, it was obviously up to me to go round to the house on the other side of the wall and say: 'Please can we have our ball back, mister?'

Thanks to enthusiastic groundsmen, who had bolted every gate in sight and patched up the various holes in the fence which had been used by countless generations for rapid access to the ground, I had to walk about a quarter of a mile to get from our side of the brick wall to the house directly on the other side of it. The whole stroll was curiously surreal: perhaps because of the heat or perhaps because it was, after all, a Sunday lunchtime, the only people I could see other than myself were Jonathan and Bart, back in the nets; there were no sounds other than their cries of triumph or distress and the snicks and thumps. Even the clouds didn't seem to be moving much. It was the kind of scene into whose description a romantic novelist would have felt impelled to insert 'Somewhere an owl hooted', if only to bring a bit of action to it.

At the end of the stroll I found the house in question; but by this time there was a definite pricking in my thumbs. Would I be attacked by a large Alsatian as I approached the front door, so that all the owners would ever hear from me would be 'I've come to ask for our . . . Aaaargh'? Or would the occupant turn out to be a beefy Sabbath-Day Observer who believed that the only sport of which the Lord approved on a Sunday was beating out the brains of would-be cricketers. These thoughts wandered in their random way through my head, and I inwardly laughed at my own paranoia – while lighting another cigarette. Then I saw the notice saying: RESIDENTIAL HOME FOR THE MENTALLY UNSTABLE.

That's funny: I seem to have one cigarette in my mouth and another in my hand.

Of course, I wasn't in the least worried. Reflecting to myself that I was probably eminently more certifiable than any of the patients in the home, I tip-toed in macho fashion up to the door and unhesitatingly got my finger to press the doorbell at only the second attempt. The idea of a meat-cleaver never crossed my mind. I stood there on the doorstep, cheerfully biting my nails, as a set of footsteps slowly approached the other side of the heavy oaken door . . . which slowly opened.

She must have been about 19 – perhaps as much as 25. She was wearing nothing but a pair of hotpants (ah – an old-fashioned girl), a skimpy, semitransparent halter, and a pair of flip-flops. She took a long, slow suck from the straw of her glass of strawberryade before she spoke to me. 'Can I help you?' she said. She flapped one flip-flop reflexively against her heel.

'It's . . . well . . . haha . . . we've been playing cricket (well, nets actually) just on the other side of your wall, and . . . heh heh . . . I know it sounds silly but . . . well, one of the balls has come over and would it be all right if I came through into your garden and found it and threw it back over the wall again and I don't want to intrude.' I was proud of that line.

'Yeah, sure. Come on through.' She led the way through the uncannily still building. She was American – or Canadian, at a guess. 'It sure is hot,' she said. 'I don't know how you guys can bear to run around with all those clothes on.'

My suave reaction was instant panic. Without saying anything, I followed her until we were standing in the garden. There, right before us, was the cricket ball. 'Thanks frightfully,' I said – frightfully.

'It's OK,' she said. 'You can climb over the wall, if you like – save you walking all that long way round. I'm gonna go back and join my boyfriend in front of the TV now. See you.'

I threw the ball over the wall and climbed up some conveniently placed gardening equipment, still thinking about *The Avengers*. What had I done wrong? In one way, I was relieved that a potential moment of embarrassment had not in fact occurred; in another, I felt rather let down – on the grounds that it would have been nice to have been *asked*. All of these inner turmoils were soon forgotten a few seconds later when I found myself straddling the inverted-V-shaped top of the wall and realizing that there was no way in which I could move either forward or back without running the severe risk of falling off and breaking my neck. 'Thank God she can't see me now,' the adolescent within me muttered mockingly. I called out very gently to Bart and Jonathan for help, and they came to help me negotiate my way down the other side.

As my eyes descended below the level of the top of the wall, as I ignominiously writhed my foot in someone's helping grasp, I saw the woman wave from an upstairs window. She was smiling in friendly fashion. Or perhaps she was simply laughing.

'That was a less than one-hundred-per-cent smooth performance on my part,' I said as I began to explain to Bart and Jonathan about what had just happened. They refused to believe me – especially half an hour later when another ball went over the wall and Bart simply shinned up it, over and back. 'I didn't see any scantily clad women,' he said with a laugh.

My wife, when I got home, was less sceptical.

'I think she was a nurse,' I said.

'She must have been.'

'What do you mean?'

'Well, if she'd been completely crazy it's just possible that she might have fancied you . . .'

Aside from all of this ego-bashing, though, the nets have gone well this year – as I've said. I've walked the three miles or so out from the centre of Newton Abbot to the pub called the 'Two Mile Oak' (*sic*), jumping into the hedge to avoid oncoming cars only two or three times a minute. Although the first match of our season has had to be cancelled, owing to bad weather, meaning that a rather uncomfortably long time has passed since I went through the full peak of my nets fitness, my shoulder still feels as if it has twice the muscular power of its winter state: I should bowl like a Michael Holding today. And, since I'm the best part of an hour early, it seems only sensible to drop into the 'Two Mile Oak' to give my shoulder – or, at least, my elbow – some exercise.

Curiously enough, our captain for the day, Mitch, and a couple of other team members have similarly decided to arrive a little early in order to ensure not being late. By some strange quirk of fate, they have just finished their drinks as I approach the table they're sitting at.

'You feeling fit?' asks Mitch a couple of minutes later as I sit down, putting my remaining threepence in my pocket.

'Yes,' I say. 'The nets really went well. I'm looking forward to shattering stumps to matchwood, and . . .'

Of course, what I really mean is that I want to bowl exactly ten balls and take with them ten wickets – something which, so far as I know, has never been done. However, taking six wickets in a single over *has* – perhaps rather more frequently than the batsman's equivalent feat of hitting six sixes in an over. This I know solely because of a feature which appeared in an edition of the award-winning science-fiction fan magazine *Xyster*, published by David Wood.

As I remarked earlier, it is downright peculiar that there should be so little of an overlap between SF people and cricket, so it was rather odd to come across this relevant item of data in an SF fanzine. It was contained in a feature which reproduced a facsimile of the correspondence columns of (at a guess) a Victorian boys' magazine. These are always particularly fascinating if the magazine concerned observed the convention of not printing the original letters, but instead only the replies of the editorial staff to those letters. The fascination arises, of course, because the mind is teased by the detective-work of trying to infer the original contents of the letter. Who or what was 'WCN', who earned the reply below?

WCN – 1. No man's debts are paid by his staying away from a town, and no man with any sense of honour would think of doing such a thing. 2. The name of her majesty was the same after her marriage as it was before, as the slightest knowledge of history would have told you. 3. We really cannot decide questions as to the amount of crape you should wear for your grandmother.

Your guess is as good as mine. And the same goes for

JOHN (Liverpool) – 1. The best exercise for you is Indian clubs. 2. Begin your letter to your master 'Sir,' and end 'Yours respectfully.'

Of rather more pertinent interest, however, is an extended answer which appears further down the column. This concerns the type of bowler whom all cricketers must envy, even if they themselves are capable of little more than turning their arms over in the nets.

A WIELDER OF THE WILLOW – Every year cases are reported of wickets being taken with every ball of an over. Last year A. Pollard, playing for Acworth School v. Badsworth, on June 26th, took six wickets with successive balls; and on August 7th W. H. Turner, playing for Egerton v. Harpurhey, performed the same feat. There were three instances of five wickets being taken with successive balls, one of them being Mr P. Carr's, for Peterhouse and Queen's v. Trinity Hall, LVC. As to four wickets with successive balls, there were six instances.

Unfortunately, I cannot identify with precision the precise year in which all these bowlers did their sterling stuff –

although it would seem to be some time after 1860. No doubt some more rigorous cricketing historian than I will be able to tell you. For my own part, I find my eyes inexorably drawn to an advertisement which appears just above this one. Has it somehow been transported through a timewarp from a twentieth-century girlie magazine to a nineteenth-century boys' journal?

RANDY – Dissolve equal parts of isinglass, alum, and soap in water, making separate solutions, and using as much water as may be necessary. Then mix the solution, and with it coat the fabric on the wrong side. Dry it, and brush it. We have often given another waterproofing solution, for which you can refer back.

One can't help wondering – to return to cricket for a moment – why it is that our ancestors were capable of all these extraordinary feats, such as taking six wickets in a single over, while in our day even the best of low-level bowlers will be only too pleased to buy everyone a pint after the match should he do so much as take a hat-trick. True, the pitches were of a lower standard in those days – but that cut both ways: all modern bowlers will tell you of the times they've sent down a perfectly directed ball, seen the batsman miss it completely, and then watched as a bump in the pitch has sent the ball over or to one side of the wicket. Could it be that our ancestors were just very poor batsmen? This is possible, because some of the scorecards from that era reveal very low scores indeed. Or could it be that those ancestors tended to exaggerate just a teensy little bit? Who knows?

Of course, mighty bowling performances still abound. A *Times* letter demonstrates this pretty conclusively:

Sir, May I record, through your columns, the occurrence of the first hat-trick, of 1985? During the annual New Year's Day match between Settle Optimists and Austwick Village (played for the ashes of the Christmas tree brought to the first ever match, now lovingly preserved in a sweet jar in the local pub) an Austwick bowler, Paul Wilson, performed this feat in his first over.

Although I was unlucky enough to be his first victim, I feel that this event is worthy of note. It took place shortly before midday at Settle (W Long. 2° 12′).

Allowing for local time differences, I wonder if your correspondents at home or abroad are aware of an earlier instance of the hat-trick this year.

Your faithfully,
Peter Metcalfe
(Secretary, Settle Optimists CC)

Today – as on any other day – I'd be quite glad to record a hat-trick, but for once in my life I'm reasonably confident that there is a chance of my doing so. In the nets, after all, I was sending them down so quickly, so accurately, so reliably . . .

I explain as much to Mitch. 'Well,' he says doubtfully, 'I suppose we could open with you and Phil; he'll go downhill and you can go uphill. The weather's not too good, so that should help you a bit. Yes, we'll get them in trouble with an initial all-pace attack.'

This is not exactly the sort of morale-boosting team-talk which David Gower gives to Norman Cowans, but it is refreshing to know that I'll be sharing the opening bowling in the first match of the new season. I flex my shoulder-muscle happily. When I put the glass down, the bunch of us start talking about Great Cricket Matches We've Played In, and Truly Diabolical Teams We've Played For; and oddly enough the conversation gets around to the team I once played for whose wicketkeeper was Dutch. He was genuinely enthusiastic about cricket – as are a lot of wealthy Dutch people, the game being something of an exclusive sport over there (rather like polo here) – but for obvious reasons he'd never learnt to play the game as a lad. The game he *had* had some experience of was hockey: in fact, he'd played at least once for Holland in the role of goalkeeper. He was, therefore, used to wearing pads and a box, and to finding hard balls flying at him at great velocities, so he was only too happy to be a 'keeper.

His technique was not, however, of the purest. Catching, for example, was not to be expected. On the other hand, he was totally fearless about the matter of getting in the way of the ball so that it wouldn't go for byes. In fact, he didn't mind which part of his body it was that got in the way of the ball. On one occasion I saw him cheerfully stop a hard new ball with his temple, his only regret being that in so doing he'd deflected it over the top of the slips for four byes.

No one around the table believes me when I talk about this fellow; instead, someone goes into the dreary, dreary rigmarole about the instructions given to foreigners as to how to play cricket. 'When the team that are in are all out, then the team that's been out go in until they're all out' – that sort of a thing. The whole set of rules is so hilariously funny that it's been reproduced everywhere; someone once even gave me a tea-towel with the words screen-printed on it.

Often I wonder if this whole business of foreigners misunderstanding cricket isn't just a little bit overdone. Every time one tries to draw up a definitive list of the countries in which cricket is played, someone comes along and points out that you've missed one; and that reminds you that you've missed another; and . . . Yet there is a strong groundswell of cricketing opinion which prefers to believe that the game is curiously and specifically *English*, that all those foreign bounders who habitually thrash the England team at Test level somehow don't really *understand* the game. No matter what the evidence placed before such bigots, they insist that the only country where cricket is played properly is England, and that cricket's rules are really quite incomprehensible to the outsider.

More likely, it is the bizarre racial intolerance of the bigoted English cricketer that the foreigners on occasion find so incomprehensible. Take this anonymous broadside which appears in John Aye's idiosyncratic little anthology, *In Praise of Cricket* (1947):

Cricket is essentially English, and though our countrymen carry it abroad wherever they go, it is difficult to inoculate or knock it into the foreigner. The Italians are too fat for cricket; the French too thin; the Dutch too dumpy; the Belgians too bilious; the Flemish too flatulent; the East Indians too peppery; the Laplanders too bow-legged; the Swiss too sentimental; the Greeks too lazy; the Egyptians too long in the neck; and the Germans too short in the wind.

All that the author really means is that, in most of the countries to which he refers, people aren't taught how to play cricket in their boy- or girlhood, like the Dutch friend whom I mentioned. This lack of youthful training is an obvious disadvantage. In countries where there is such a tradition cricket prospers at both a national and an international level. One wonders why the anonymous writer failed to mention Australia, or New Zealand, or the West Indies, and why he felt that the people of the East Indies were 'too peppery' to play cricket competently. The answer is, of course, that like so many of us he had fixed upon his theory – that only the English can play cricket – and was resolutely determined to ignore any evidence which might contradict it.

Of course, there can be problems in playing cricket in countries outside the British Isles. There's the wellknown tale – how true it is I do not know – of the Australian schoolboy who in 1967 was batting in a practice match when he saw a metre-long poisonous snake gliding across the greensward towards him. A plucky lad, he ignored the ball which had just been bowled to him and went to club the creature to death with his bat. Surprised not to hear great cries of delight from the wicketkeeper behind him, he turned around to discover that, after all, he was in no danger whatsoever of being stumped: the 'keeper had long since decided to display the better part of valour.

Also well known is the legend of the Indian or Pakistani boundary fielder whose cricketing career ended when, during the course of one match, he was inadvertently eaten by a tiger.

Less depressingly, cricket overseas can create difficulties of a more minor kind. In January 1985 there was played what is believed to be the most southerly cricket match of all time – in Antarctica, some 400 miles north of the South Pole – between two teams designated the Beardmore Casuals and the Gondwanaland Occasionals. Simon Barnes, who reported the occasion in his excellent 'Sporting Diary' in the London *Times*, did not tell us any details of the score, but he did provide other fascinating data:

A heavy roller in the form of a Hercules transport aircraft was applied but the pitch took spin from the start, said Arthur Watts, captain of Beardmore. The players – scientists, lawyers, diplomats and environmentalists from 13 nations attending the Antarctic Treaty Conference – found conditions tricky and 13 of them returned frozen, despite playing in thermal clothing and snowboots.

Clearly the report caused some controversy among *Times* readers, because a week later Barnes was driven to mention what was, by contrast, probably the most northerly cricket match ever played – at a latitude of 77° 20′ in

Spitsbergen in 1894. An additional interesting feature of this match was that, thanks to the fact that it was played north of the Arctic Circle, it was carried on right through the midnight hour.

Of course, it is true that there are a few people outside the cricketing nations who have some little difficulty in understanding the ethos of the game. It is reported that in the 1840s someone took Ibraham Pasha, son of Egypt's Mehemet Ali, along to a cricket match at Lord's. After watching the game for a couple of hours, the royal visitor finally, in desperation, sent a message out to the two captains: without wanting to hurry them unnecessarily, he would be grateful if they could stop all this aimless running around and start actually playing the game.

By far and away the best book to consult on the subject of the foreign attitude to cricket is Allen Synge's anthology *Strangers' Gallery* (1974), and in it we find a genuine version of the rules of cricket as explained to non-cricketing peoples. The writer is the *Izvestia* correspondent V. Osipov, who told an adoring Soviet public that

The game itself seems somewhat like our *lapta*. There is a beautifully maintained ground. There are eleven attackers and eleven defenders. The attackers perform as a whole team together. The defenders have two 'batsmen' in at a time, and their job is to hit the ball delivered by the opponents' 'bowler' at a little gate (wicket) of three vertical columns (about the size of the bat in our game of *gorodki*) with a small bar on top (like the block in *gorodki*). While the players in the field belonging to the attacking side chase after the ball the man who has hit it should exchange places with his partner. Each successful hit means points, and a first-class batsman can hold off an attack for hours on end and the match itself carry on for a week.

There, that's perfectly clear. Isn't it?

Cricket has its supporters in other countries, too – even

in some of the more unexpected ones, like France and the United States of America. Granted, cricketers in those countries tend to be rather rare birds – and often, too, they are merely British people who have emigrated. So it's mildly pleasing to note that in 1908 it was an American who came at the top of the English first-class bowling averages. He was a certain John B. King, who played for a touring side called the Gentlemen of Philadelphia. In that year he succeeded in taking no fewer than 87 wickets at a perfectly respectable average of 11.01.

So far as I know, there haven't been any equally distinguished cricketers from France – but that is not to say that the game is not played there. Indeed, by one of those curious quirks of fate, the only time that cricket has been included as one of the sports in an Olympic Games was in 1900, when the Games were held as a sort of side-attraction to the Paris Exposition of that year. In fact, the Games were so much of a side-attraction that it was not until 1965 that one French cyclist who had taken part realized that he was the proud owner of an Olympic silver medal. The records of these, the second Olympic Games of the new cycle, are in some chaos; but we do know, for example, that they marked the entrance of women to the Games (lawn tennis), and we also know some of the results – which suggest that the athletic standard was not in general as high as one might expect. The American called Baxter who took the gold medal in the pole vault, for instance, and who equalled the then Olympic record of 10ft 10in in so doing, actually performed a jump over five feet less than the *qualifying* standard for a modern Olympiad.

One of the other results of which we know concerns Britain's gold-medal-winning performance in the cricketing contest – and Britain remains the champion in the event to this day!

Well, not quite.

The truth of the matter is that C. B. K. Beachcroft led a team across to Paris for the event, but in fact it wasn't really a British team: it was the Devon County Wanderers. The only match which they had to play in order to win the little-coveted trophy was one against an All-Paris XII which seems, as far as we can judge from the scorecard, to have been made up of British expatriates. The other thing that we can gather from the scorecard is that it was not, shall we say, the most distinguished of matches. There were twelve players on each side, and the match lasted for two days, but the scores were not especially high. In fact, no complete scorecard exists, although it is believed that Montague Toller, the Devonian fast bowler, took 7 wickets for 9 or 10 runs – no mean feat. The batting was as follows:

Devon County Wanderers: First Innings

C. B. K. Beachcroft b. Attrill	23
A. D. Birkett b. Anderson	1
J. Symes c. Anderson b. Robinson	15
F. W. Cuming c. Browning b. McEvoy	38
M. H. Toller b. McEvoy	2
A. Bowerman b. Anderson	7
A. J. Powlesland c. Browning b. Robinson	10
W. S. Sonne run out	0
F. W. Christian b. Anderson	6
G. J. Buckley b. Attrill	2
F. R. Burchell not out	0
H. R. Corner lbw b. Anderson	4
Extras	9
TOTAL	117

This is the sort of total which, at our level, would cause a certain amount of unease on the part of both captains:

it's not really big enough to be safe, on the one hand, but
then – on the other – it's big enough for it not to be a
foregone conclusion that the opposition can surpass it. In
fact, as it proved, Beachcroft need not have worried too
much. The All-Paris team's first innings looked like this:

All-Paris XII: First Innings

T. H. Jordan c. Corner b. Christian	11
A. J. Schneidau b. Christian	8
R. Horne c Buckley b. Christian	15
H. Terry c. Cuming b. Powlesland	2
F. Roques b. Powlesland	0
W. Anderson b. Christian	0
D. Robinson b. Christian	0
W. T. Attrill lbw b. Christian	0
W. Browning b. Christian	0
A. McEvoy b. Bowerman	1
P. H. Tomalin n.o.	3
J. Braid run out	25
Extras	13
TOTAL	78

It's interesting to notice that the Devon County Wanderers' star bowler, Toller, features not at all in the tally
of dismissals in the All-Paris first innings. After all, he
had played half a dozen times for Somerset (in 1897) as
well as putting in regular appearances for Devon. It
seems more than likely that his captain, Beachcroft, had
decided to hold Toller back in order to make more of a
contest of it.

Still, the Devon County Wanderers were far from safe.
They had a lead of 39 runs on the first innings, but that's
the sort of margin that a good partnership (inspired,
perhaps, by that twelfth man, J. Braid) can soon wipe

out. Clearly they had to do some good work with the bat in the second innings if they were to have any chance of being safe. And time was passing . . .

Devon County Wanderers: Second Innings

C. B. K. Beachcroft run out	54
J. Symes c. Attrill b. Roques	1
F. W. Cuming c. Attrill b. McEvoy	18
A. Bowerman b. Roques	59
H. R. Corner n.o.	5
Extras	9
TOTAL (for 5 wickets declared)	145

The Devon County Wanderers were 184 runs ahead which, judging by the All-Paris XII's performance in the first innings, must have made them feel pretty secure. On the other hand, so that the match didn't end as a draw, they had actually to bowl out the All-Paris XII for the second time. Presumably it was at this moment that Beachcroft, anxious to escape the draw, decided to use his master-weapon, Toller. Parisophiles should decline to read the next few lines.

T. H. Jordan b. Toller	0
A. J. Schneidau b. Powlesland	1
R. Horne b. Powlesland	1
H. Terry b. Toller	1
F. Roques b. Toller	0
W. Anderson b. Toller	8
D. Robinson b. Powlesland	0
W. T. Attrill b. Toller	0
W. Browning b. Toller	0
A. McEvoy c. Christian b. Corner	0
P. H. Tomalin n.o.	6
J. Braid b. Toller	7
Extras	2
TOTAL	**26**

And so the Devonians had won the gold medal for Britain by 158 runs – a suitably convincing victory – although one should add that they did so with only about five minutes to spare. Had J. Braid, that excellent number twelve, been able to block for just a little while longer . . .

If the French and the Americans can play cricket, then there seems no reason why the Scottish cannot, too. Nevertheless, the cricket-is-exclusively-English fraternity still raise their collective eyebrows whenever I announce in the pub after a match, actually, um, I learnt how to play cricket in Scotland. Not even at a Scottish public school – although it was at just such an establishment that I learnt that cricketers were supposed to do things like wear white clothes – but amongst buddies playing in decrepit nets left erect in a local Aberdeen park presumably because the city council couldn't afford to send a gardener to take the damn' things down.

But the cricketing tradition in Scotland is of reasonable strength; an aunt of mine who lives on Clydeside can well remember the many times she went to watch Greenock Cricket Club playing. In part the tradition is due to the influence of the Scottish public schools, which try to be at least as English as the English public schools and preferably more so; in rather larger part, I think, it is due to the fact that cricket is an absorbing game which can be played just as well on Scottish pitches as it can on English. Whatever the truth of the matter might be, the tradition, as I say, exists – and nowhere more so than in those Scottish public schools, on the one hand, and in the southern border country, on the other.

Andrew Lang, probably best known for his collections of fairy stories, which reflected his activities as an avid researcher of Scottish folklore, experienced Scottish cricket in both 'areas'. He wrote about the game with infectious enthusiasm in an essay entitled 'Border Cricket', which first appeared in 1904 in the cricketing volume of the *Badminton Library of Sports and Pastimes*, although it appears that the essay was written a good few years earlier. He shows in the essay all the true characteristics of the genuine cricket *player*, as opposed to passive spectator: a total disinterest in the larger events of state and a total fascination with the events of the matches in which *he* has played. To wit:

The most exciting match, I think, in which I ever took part was for Loretto [public school] against another school. When our last man went in, second innings, we were still four runs behind our opponents' first score. This last man was extremely short-sighted, and the game seemed over. But his partner, a very steady player, kept the bowling, and put on some thirty-eight more. We put our adversaries in to get this, and had lowered eight wickets for twenty-eight. I was bowling, and appealed to the umpire of our opponents for a palpable catch at wicket. 'Not out!' Next ball the batsman was caught at long-stop, and a fielder triumphantly shouted, 'Well, how's *that?*'

'Not out', replied the professional again, and we lost the match by two wickets.

If this had happened on the Border, there would have been trouble, and perhaps the two clubs would not have met again for years. . . .

It seems that in Lang's time cricketers in the Scottish border country displayed a certain earnestness, an eagerness to win at all costs, which did not 'invariably promote the friendliness of a friendly game'. The team in which he himself played was 'a kind of family team', containing a few adults plus lots of younger brothers, so that 'very small children would occasionally toddle up and bowl when the elder members of the family were knocked off [i.e., out]'. However, by the natural course of things, the small children eventually turned into larger ones, until the team developed into what was at that time the only wandering club in the borders, 'The Eccentric Flamingoes'.

We wore black and red curiously disposed, and had a good many Oxford members. The Flamingoes, coming down from Oxford, full of pride, had once a dreadful day on the Edinburgh Academy Ground. We were playing the school, which made a portentous score, and I particularly remember that Mr T. R. Marshall, probably the best Scotch bat who ever played, and then a boy, hit two sixes and a five off consecutive balls. It is a very great pity that this Border bat is so seldom seen at Lord's; his average for MCC in 1886 was 85. The Flamingoes lasted for some years, and played all Teviotdale and Tweedside.

There is, of course, still an official Scottish national side, although sadly it seems to get hammered every time it plays an English county. The same is true of the most curious 'national' side of all – that of the Palmerston Islands. The self-appointed government-in-exile of this group of atolls in the Pacific now resides in Finland, although it would be rather churlish to say that its members are in fact Finnish. On two occasions their 'country' has taken on a representative English team – made up of members of the British Embassy in Helsinki, and so on. According to Kari Kyheröinen, one of the members of the Palmerston Islands team (writing in Synge's *Strangers' Gallery*), both matches resulted in an English victory. In the first, the English triumph was by a total, over two innings, of 110 to 60; in the second, where bad weather stopped play after the first innings, the English side was leading by a margin of 60 runs to 31. Very sportingly, the Palmerston Islanders decided to concede this as a defeat.

In the same general part of the world as the Palmerston Islands is the French territory, New Caledonia, which genuinely does have a strong cricketing tradition. The rules are rather different: the soft ball is not so much bowled as thrown, all batsmen have runners, and there are 13 players to a full team. Perhaps the biggest difference, however, is in the relative degrees of involvement of the sexes in New Caledonian cricket: at the last count there were about 4400 registered cricketers in the territory, and of these just over 3000 were women. Perhaps sadly, the current government of New Caledonia has plans to reverse the relative importance of male and female cricket by bringing in outside coaches to try to generate a national male side of sufficient calibre to take on some of the more traditional cricketing countries.

Of course, the cricket-is-nothing-if-not-English brigade will discount these few randomly selected examples of its being played in diverse scattered places. They will point to the differences in rules, such as those noted in New Caledonia. But I don't think that this argument holds water. Not so long ago I was passing a local school when I heard the traditional cries you associate with a cricket match in progress – 'Come on. No – stay – stay – wait – yes, *come on*.' Having a few minutes to spare, I found a convenient hole in the hedge and peered through.

Sure enough, the boys were playing cricket. Well, perhaps not exactly the same game as you or I might play. They were dressed in white shirts and shorts, and they were using what looked to me, from the distance, to be a fives ball (it was smaller than a rounders ball). For bats they were using table-tennis bats, held in that style whereby the thumb goes across the face of the bat. The pitch was perhaps ten to fifteen yards long, and the bowling consisted of a gentle underarm toss from the games-master. You could be run out or caught out, but you couldn't be bowled or stumped (I don't think) because in place of a wicket there was a sort of scaffolding affair with a square of white hardboard attached to it. The bowling was one way only, and there seemed to be no such thing as an over, because, as I've said, the only bowler was the games-master. Otherwise, the rules seemed to be roughly the same as in more conventional cricket.

Still, you may feel, they were playing a game *based* on cricket, but it wasn't actually a game of cricket. But that's the curious thing about it: it very definitely *was* cricket. It wasn't, for example, a distorted version of rounders. The atmosphere was that of any other school cricket match; the evident emotions of the players were cricketing emotions; the ethics observed were cricket's. In a curious kind of a way, it was an identical game, but with the rules changed – if that isn't too paradoxical for you.

With rather a lot of the rules changed, you may feel – and that's exactly my point. In New Caledonia, for example, only a very few of the rules have been changed. All right, so the teams are XIIIs rather than XIs – but it is only in comparatively recent times that XI has become the universal norm, and there are still plenty of five- or seven-a-side cricket games played in all the traditional cricketing countries. All right, so the balls used are soft, but so they are in lots of cricket games in this country among the very young (I don't mean just in beach cricket). In short, there is no reason to believe that the cricket in New Caledonia or wherever is any less cricket than the unusual game I came across in that local school. As in so many more weighty matters, we should be looking for international similarities rather than crowing about international differences. I couldn't disagree more with H. A. Vachell, when he said in his *The Best of England*:

Who was the wag who said that England was separated from the rest of the world by an immense gulf called cricket? It is a true and witty saying. Very few foreigners understand or like our great national game, to which it might be retorted that very few of them understand or like us. In a sense cricket is – US. It stands for what we practise and preach – concerted action, team play, the discipline of the individual, the recognition of authority, and the subservience of all to the common end.

That may have been true once upon a time, but it's certainly not true now. Perhaps not at governmental or diplomatic level, but at the level of the average member of the cricketing fraternity, be he or she player or spectator, cricket serves to form a powerful bond between people of many nations: probably the favourite 'local boy' in the county of Somerset is Viv Richards, or Joel Garner, or, especially, Hallam Moseley. Moreover, to say that cricket reflects all that is truly English – 'concerted action, team play, the discipline of the individual, the recognition of authority, and the subservience of all to the common end' – is to paint a smug and basically false picture of what English social behaviour is really like. These days, in real life as opposed to cricket matches, the very idea of 'team play', for example, is virtually heretical: the pursuit of personal greed has been glorified. 'Recognition of authority' is not a universally popular notion in modern England, either – sometimes, although not always, because that authority is being abused. And one cannot really make a case that 'once upon a time' all the qualities of which Vachell talks were fundamental elements of what the English actually practised – although the English may well have *preached* them, and thereby helped spread some valuable notions.

No, cricket does not epitomize the codes of behaviour of England or of any other country . . . except a utopia. Cricket's ethics are those to which we *should* subscribe in everyday life (to be fair, to which some people do), much in the same way that so many of us believe that we should adhere to the Christian moral code but so rarely do. We need not be either Christians or cricketers to recognize that we ought to be behaving in those ways – and we certainly need not be English.

Utopias are, after all, international.

Many of these reflections are bandied about the table as further pints are sunk. By this time it is nearing quarter past two, and most of our side are here. It is time to stroll up the road a couple of hundred yards to the little Abbotskerswell pitch, which features quite often in these pages, it being the nearest thing we have to a home ground. The opposition are already there, skulking around outside the pavilion, looking out at the damp day with a mixture of depression and glee. It's probably their first match of the season, too, and that's always a case for general rejoicing; but it would be nice if the weather were just a little bit more welcoming. There is absolutely no question, of course, of calling the match off. Even were it raining – which it isn't, quite – we would go ahead.

The keys appear from somewhere, and the business of changing gets underway. The ribald remarks start up as if there had been no gap of a few months since last we went through this ritual. Willy has still not washed or pressed his trousers, which someone suggests are still bearing traces of mud from Waterloo. Vince says that he's going to give the club's new Jumbo bat its first airing, and there's an immediate cry of 'Did you say "Jumbo" or "Dumbo"?' As usual, I just quietly get into my whites as swiftly as possible; I want to go through the traditional rite of scrabbling a ball out of the bag and tossing it high in the air to catch it – or not, as the case may be. Despite the sogginess of the atmosphere, I can smell cricket in it. I want to be out there, throwing and running and catching and bowling – most of all bowling.

It is at this point that my shoelace breaks. In the ordinary way this would not be too much of a disaster; I would simply make do with the longer of the two pieces and throw the shorter one away. Unfortunately, that's what I did the last time, in September, and the time before that. Each of the two remaining fragments is only a few inches long – far too short to hold my shoe onto my foot with any conviction.

A good game of cricket obviously does not depend on good-quality equipment, but equally obviously it helps if your garments and kit are not disintegrating all around you. Still, one must make do as best one can. My solution is to take the lace off my other shoe and snap it in half – which, bearing in mind that its partner has broken so many times, proves remarkably hard to do. Still, I end up with two half-laces which are just long enough to serve – although it's going to be an absolute bloody disaster if either of them goes, as Rudolph remarks with pleasure.

Fingers crossed.

Roy Hattersley, in an essay in his collection *Politics Apart* (1982), recalls with a mixture of affection and bitter hatred his first two pairs of cricket boots – back in the days when cricket boots were hefty things rather than the modern ballet pumps. The young Hattersley's first boots, a pair of size tens picked up in a local junkshop, proved to be a more than merely generous fit on his youthful size-seven feet – but for a while he loved them.

They had been made in canvas, but by the time they came into my possession they had developed the patina of parchment and were as supple as pre-stressed concrete. The tin eyelet holes had been torn from their moorings, so the laces meandered unguided across my feet while the sharp edges of the uppers cut into my ankle bones. Worst of all, the soles were so withered and dry that they would not hold the steel studs that we used to cling to in the age before special turf-gripping extruded surfaces were invented.

Cricket gear does seem to age in a curious way. In the old days a good bat might be passed down for generations, getting if anything better and better as time went on. Nowadays, the average bat bought by our club (as opposed to the individual bats bought by some of the better – and worse – batsmen) lasts at best about two or three seasons before either breaking completely or just becoming as dead as a dodo. One or two of our side, recognizing this, have bought old-fashioned bats second-hand. It has become something of a trend, though, to 'improve' these. Jonathan started it all by scooping out much of the back of his bat, so that it weighed a lot less without any loss of 'meat'. His experiment proved to be successful, so Ronnie picked up a dreadful old bat from somewhere for about fifty pence – he wuz robbed – and tampered with it in similar fashion; he christened the resulting implement 'Ballbuster'. When he speculated out loud as to whether or not his efforts would have affected the qualities of the bat, it was pointed out acidly that we'd have to wait a few weeks until he actually succeeded in hitting the ball to find out.

Like bats, some gloves can improve with age – although this is not often appreciated. Our club bag contains the usual mixture of new, stiff, sausage-fingered pairs and old, disreputable-looking ones with holes in the canvas palms. Every now and then someone will complain that these tatty old specimens are simply taking up valuable space in a bag that is already bulging, and be surprised when there is a great cry of protest at the very suggestion of getting rid of them. My favourite pair is one of those with green, spiky rubber bits along the backs of the fingers; in fact, these spiky bits are virtually the only part of the gloves still to survive. A couple of us did try a year or two ago to buy a replacement pair of this type of gloves but were everywhere told that they weren't stocked by sports shops because there was no demand for them; everyone wanted the sausage-fingered type. Our pleas that there *was* a demand for the spiky ones, because here were we demanding them, fell on deaf ears.

Boots are different from bats and gloves, though: they don't age in the same way at all. A single cricketer can wear the same pair of boots for decades, and if anything they'll improve slightly over the years. But if he tries to pass on his boots to his son, say, the result is disastrous – even if both of them have the same size of feet. Not only will the new wearer be in agony most of the time, his performance will be markedly damaged for reasons unknown other than those associated with the fact that his feet are hurting like hell. Quite why this should be I don't know – after all, people can pass on pairs of ordinary shoes without too much trouble.

After a while with his first pair of boots, Roy Hattersley decided that he needed something better if he were going to have much chance of opening the batting for Yorkshire. Once again, he was forced by financial constraints to purchase his next pair second-hand, but they did seem initially to be something of an improvement.

They were, as I proudly pointed out to anyone who would listen, made of real leather. As an aid to deep-sea diving they would have been invaluable. . . . I never realized that for two years I batted for Wadsley Church, the City Grammar School and Sheffield YMCA in white-painted hobnailed boots.

Simply carrying them to the grounds used up most of my day's energy. The only benefit they bestowed upon my batting was the protection that they provided against stumping. My feet were permanently anchored inside the crease.

My own first boots were of similar massiveness, but most of the weight was concentrated in the thick solid-leather heels. The soles were by contrast quite thin, so that I had to be careful about which brand of studs I used for them: any but the shortest would go right through to give a little alpine range of sharp points which cut mercilessly into my feet. Perhaps for this reason, I was constantly losing studs, and hammering in replacements was no joke, because the boots had been carefully designed so that they could not be held still as the stud was struck in. By the time the soles of the boots were beginning to look rather like a colander, with very few areas of intact leather to take further studs, I got fed up with the whole process, and for a few weeks didn't bother replacing any that fell out. Then I noticed that, despite the studlessness of my boots, I seemed not to be falling over in the field any more than usual, and so I never put another stud in them.

They were still pretty heavy boots, though. One day,

when I couldn't lay hands on them in a hurry, I made do with a pair of white gymshoes, and found that I was moving over the greensward at a rather swifter pace than my habitual slow-motion waddle; so ever since I have earned the disapproving glances of the keenies by sticking to white gymshoes. Their only disadvantage is that, when the ground underfoot is wet and slippery, I'm likely to do a dramatic skid as I let go of the ball when bowling – but then in those circumstances virtually *any* footwear but a pair of rugby boots is going to be less than perfect.

People's first bats are usually lumps of driftwood, picked up on the beach and used to thrash a light rubber ball about; or they may be those imitation cricket bats which are sold along with four stumps and a set of bails as a children's cricket set. At a very slightly higher level are the ones generally bought from Woolworth's, and made in Pakistan, which have genuine splices (although little lumps of glue extrude along the lines of the splice); they also have knot-holes and no detectable 'meat', and always seem rather smaller when you start trying to play with them than they did in the shop. And then there's the home-made bat. In his modern classic of cricket, *The Best Loved Game* (1979), Geoffrey Moorhouse recalls with obvious affection the primitive equipment he used in his boyhood:

I used to spend hours in the field beside our house with a rubber ball and a home-made bat, whose handle was fashioned from an old carpet-beater, with a bicycle inner tube rolled double down to the shoulder of the blade, which had once been a mahogany shelf.

He fails to give any details of its performance character-istics, but I think we can guess them.

* * *

Soon most of us are outside chucking a ball around. We do not do this as professionally as the opposition, but this doesn't worry us much – we so seldom do. Half of us have cigarettes drooping from our mouths as we go through the motions of fielding practice, although Godfrey brings a touch of style to the proceedings by smoking a cigar instead. What starts as a gentle chuck-around degenerates, as always, into one of those contests in which the fielders stand as far apart as they can throw, sending the ball high and swooping across the full width of the circle and shouting with glee as their fellows yell with pain at their stinging palms and staved fingers. At one point, as I'm throwing the ball across to Jonathan, I feel a twinge in my shoulder which is obviously slightly rusty after its enforced fortnight's idleness. Still, the muscle seems to be working all right; just a little twinge.

Mitch wins the toss and tells us that he's decided to field first – to my great delight. Phil and I go out to take a look at the strip, which seems in pretty good condition, although it's a bit slippery around where one will be going into one's delivery stride. I scent wickets.

Phil's first over is the usual sort of first over produced by a fast bowler in the first match of the season: a couple of good balls, a couple of bad ones, and a couple of nondescript ones. The batsman looks in no danger whatsoever of being out, but the honours are probably roughly equal, because he is unable to take a run off Phil, and a couple of times plays and misses by a very wide margin.

At the end of the over I take the ball cockily; if only Phil had done a bit more net practice he might have taken a wicket there, but as it is he's left it to me. I pace out my run-up, decide that for safety's sake I'll start running in from my mark rather than, as usual, from a few yards behind it, set the field with Mitch, and prepare to begin. As I run in I can feel the cold air singing through my hair and pouring coldly into my lungs. This is it – the start of the season – the first ball I've bowled outside the nets for some six months – the moment I've been looking forward to all through the winter . . .

But what's this? My rhythm is perfect, I reach the delivery crease at exactly the right velocity and in the perfect bodily configuration, but as my arm comes over there is a feeling of absolute and complete powerlessness in my shoulder muscle. The ball goes looping slowly through the air and is still at well over head-height as it passes above the batsman to descend into the gloves of our 'keeper. The umpire, quite rightly, signals a wide – although I note with a smile to him that about the one kind word you could say about the performance was that at least I'd got my line right: the ball went straight over the top of the middle stump . . . some six feet over the top of middle stump, but still . . .

The next ball is a repeat of the first. 'Sorry about this,' I say to Mitch. 'I can't understand what's going on. I'm not slipping, or anything.'

'You keep going until you find your rhythm,' he says charitably.

'It's not my rhythm,' I say. 'It's my bloody arm.'

'Keep going anyway. Try bowling off a short run-up.'

By the time I finish my first over the opposition score is ticking along quite merrily, although neither batsmen has yet taken a run – possibly because they've been unable to reach most of the deliveries I've sent down. I apologize again to Mitch: 'I've done something to my shoulder. You'd better take me off. Perhaps after I've done some fielding it'll pull its socks up.'

He looks deeply disappointed in me. After all his cheery remarks about a pace attack, he has Phil bowling at less than his best (although still quite well) and me bowling about as effectively as my seven-year-old daughter. 'No,' he says, 'take another over and see how it goes.'

My second over – and my last of the day – is even longer than the first. At a guess, I must have sent down 12 or 14 deliveries in order to complete my six legitimate ones; now I'm skulking around on the boundary feeling a prickling in my eyes. It's not just a matter of damaged pride; I'm also extremely worried. Of course, I've strained my shoulder countless times in the past, and have known the consequent pain and powerlessness as I've completed the requisite number of deliveries to get to the end of the over. But, aside from that slight twinge just before the game, I've had no pain today in the muscle, and I know that I haven't pulled it.

And, in due course, we lose the match quite convincingly. I take the blame personally, of course; and even as we carouse in the bar afterwards I feel overpoweringly guilty while at the same time worrying myself sick about my shoulder. Somebody suggests a game of darts to me, and I jokingly point out that that would be a criminally dangerous idea on my part; but inside I'm not laughing.

'Tendonitis,' says the doctor the following morning, and instinctively I translate this into layperson's language: 'Buggered tendons.' The doctor continues: 'There's only one way of getting rid of it. I'll give you a course of tablets, but they won't work unless you give your shoulder a rest for three or four weeks. You can play cricket if you want to, but field close in, so that you don't have to do much throwing, and above all don't bowl.'

As I leave the surgery I think that the 1984 cricket season is really and truly under way, with our first match having been played. Twenty-four hours ago the thought would have had me dancing and kicking my heels along the pavement, but now it is slowly and sadly that I make my way down to the chemist's to exchange my prescription.

5

THE SCRATCH MATCH

12th August, 1984

'I just love it!' says Jonathan through a mouthful of lager. 'Here it is Wednesday, and those bastards from the *Barchester Chronicle* have only just 'phoned up to say that they can't muster a team for Sunday. Where the hell are we going to find someone to play against at this short notice? Swine.'

Mentally I bowdlerize his language and substitute '*Barchester Chronicle*' for the name of the Plymouth-based newspaper whose cricketers are letting us down. 'Dunno,' I say helpfully.

'Bastards,' says Vince.

'I've 'phoned a couple of people,' Jonathan continues moodily, his eyes straying reflexively to the jeans-clad bottom of a passing person whose mind he longs to admire, 'but they say their teams are already booked up for Sunday. Hardly surprising. We're just going to have to call the whole thing off.'

'That'd be a shame,' I say. 'The weather's so beautiful at the moment. If Sunday's like this it'd be a positive crime not to have a game of cricket.'

'What makes it worse,' says Jonathan, 'is that we've already paid for the ground. I suppose I could try to find someone who'd be willing to sublet it from us, but that's a bit unlikely, too.'

'We could ask the *Exeter Weekly News* to run a little story for us,' I say. 'You know, Local Team Seeks Fixture – that sort of a thing. Last season there was this touring side down from Hampshire, or somewhere, half of whose people had had to go home early, and the *Weekly Snooze* ran a wee piece saying they were desperate for volunteers. They got enough players, all right.'

'Yes,' says Vince, 'but look at the standard of volunteers they got. You were one of them.'

'I'll have a pint,' I counter, squashing him effectively.

While Vince is up at the bar, exchanging winks, giggles and nudges with a bored-looking barmaid, I have what I think might be an inspiration. 'Would you like me to give Jim a ring?' I say. 'I might be able to persuade him to raise a Devonair team to give us a match.'

'The last time we tried to play a game with Devonair they had to drop out at the last minute,' says Jonathan. 'Couldn't get a team together.'

'Well, I could suggest to Jim that he try and ask some people along from Radio Devon, too, to make up the numbers.' Devonair is the local independent radio station, and has been on the air for some years. I'm very fond of the station, because I like the people there – they have been very good to me, one way and another. Radio Devon, the BBC's reply to Devonair, is by contrast much newer and is as yet something of a closed book to me. Jim, who is now in charge of light entertainment or something at Devonair, worked for a few months at Radio Devon and – a while before – for Devonair, with the overall result that he has interviewed me on the air more than anyone else. Also, he knows most of the people involved in radio in this neck of the woods. If anyone's likely to be able to get a team together at short notice, Jim is.

'OK,' says Jonathan, 'you 'phone Jim this afternoon. Let me know what happens.' His voice lacks conviction.

But Jim comes through – although he stresses to me that the team he's going to assemble can in no way be described as a Devonair team – or even a Broadcasting XI: it's simply a side made up of friends of his who're prepared to turn out and wave the bat. I ask him nervously if, er, he'll make sure that he doesn't bring along too many top-rate players. 'No worry,' he cries. 'They're all about the same standard as me.'

Jim has played for us once. He went in at number three, having told us all he was a batsman. He was clean bowled first ball. 'That sounds ideal,' I say.

And so it is that a few days later we find ourselves all at the Abbotskerswell ground, chatting with the friends that Jim's brought with him. They are a motley bunch – it's not just that some of them aren't in whites, but that a number of them are in blue shorts and flip-flops. By the workings of Grant's Second Law (discussed on page 184), we are in for a pulverizing. Still, they're a friendly bunch of people: that's what counts.

'These Devonair people look like a load of wallies,' says Willy. 'We should stuff them.'

If ever confirmation had been needed that we were going to lose ignominiously, this is it. When Willy reckons that the opposition's going to be useless, they infallibly turn out to be first-rate. The curious thing is that, after-wards, as he looks at the scorebook to see that we managed to muster a score only just into double figures, while failing to get any of their batsmen out in a total of over 200, he never admits that perhaps his prediction was at fault: we'd have beaten them if we'd had a full-strength team, or if they hadn't brought along a couple of high-class ringers, or . . . 'And anyway,' I say, 'they're not a Devonair team. They're a Jim Paxton Invitation XI.' The protest will prove to be useless: all afternoon our people will insist on referring to the opposition as 'Devonair'. I suppose they think it's more glamorous to be playing against Media People – wow.

'What's the betting they have someone really good with them,' says Bart, eager as ever to see Willy put his foot in it. Actually, Bart is probably correct: sure as eggs, scratch teams usually turn out to have somebody who's a brilliant player. I'm reminded of the army batsman Major A. C. Richards, who during an illustrious career played for Hertfordshire and Hampshire. It was when playing for an army team, however, that he brought off his most astonishing feat. E Company, for which he was playing against A Company in 1901 at Barberton, scored 114 in the first innings, of which he made 101, and 221 in the second, of which he scored 185; in other words, ignoring extras, he got 286 out of the 311 that E Company scored off the bat. As if this were not enough to convince A Company that someone, somewhere, had cheated by bringing along a player from a different level of the game, Richards took 8 of the wickets to fall in the first A Company innings. The highest score from any other E Company batsman was . . . 6!

Nobody else has ever heard of Major A. C. Richards, so halfway through my anecdote I shut up and concentrate on changing into my kit.

By contrast with the men in the shorts and flip-flops, one or two of Jim's team are superbly turned out: white flannel trousers with razor-sharp creases, new-looking white shirts, real cricket boots sparkling with freshly applied blanco – the works. The only person in our team with razor creases in his trousers, apart from Godfrey, is, as usual, Willy. The only trouble is, the creases in Willy's trousers are legion, criss-crossing the cloth every which way. The trousers haven't seen the inside of a washing-machine for more years than most of us would care to remember, and seem to be stored, crumpled, under a heavy weight. Willy is very proud of them.

He certainly wouldn't have been allowed to play for the film actor Sir C. Aubrey Smith. Smith was an exceptionally keen cricketer – in fact, once upon a time he had captained England – and so it was hardly surprising that, when he got to Hollywood, he should organize a cricket club there. This club was not, as you might have expected, simply an excuse for expatriate Brits to congregate for an afternoon of drinking and horseplay in the sun: Smith demanded the highest possible standards of play, dress and decorum.

So it was especially tragic when, one day, he committed the sin of sins: he dropped a comparatively simple catch in the slips. Before anyone could ever so gently hint that this was the very crime for which he had so often in the past castigated the other players, he called for his butler, who was commanded sternly to fetch his master's spectacles.

These were brought out to him on a silver salver, and Smith put them on, rubbed his hands in professional fashion, and settled back into his position at slip. Play was resumed and, sure enough, the very next ball was snicked, shot into the slips, and was put down by the actor himself. There was a tense pause before this screen aristocrat *par excellence* shouted bitterly to an unheeding Fate: 'Egad! The damned fool brought me my *reading* glasses!'

Of course, the upper crust have often dabbled in lesser-grade cricket. Possibly the upper-crustiest of the lot of them was George IV, who was a keen, and – it seems – reasonably good cricketer. While he was still Regent he disguised himself on one occasion to play a match against a certain cobbler who was widely reported to be a fearsome bowler. The prince resisted the hostile bowling for a while, but in the end his centre stump went down. Being the Prince Regent, he had a mild tantrum about this, but after he had calmed down a bit he went so far as to give the cobbler some money, and later he invited the man to come to Windsor. The future George IV is reported as having said, by way of justification: 'If the man can make shoes as well as he can play cricket, he shall be my cobbler.'

Some years earlier, when the prince would have been only six years old, the adventurer and petty crook William Hickey played for a team of old boys at Westminster School against a team of Eton old boys in a match which had been organized by the Duke of Dorset; Hickey, although he was in disgrace for having been caught embezzling, was in demand for his skill as a wicket-keeper. The night before the match, however, he fell in with some loose friends, who got him drunk and robbed him. He awoke in the chill dawn, somehow remembered his obligation to play cricket, and ordered a coach home.

. . . I vomited out of the coach window the whole way, to the great entertainment of the foot passengers.

On my arrival home, the servants were shocked to see the condition I was in, looking pale as a corpse. They strenuously recommended my going to bed, but that I declared absolutely impossible, as I must be at Moulsey in little more than an hour. The clearing my stomach of the vile stuff it contained had in some measure relieved me, though I still had an excruciating headache. Whilst changing my clothes, the servants prepared some very strong coffee, which proved of infinite benefit. Having washed, put on clean linen, and had my hair dressed, I again stepped into the same coach that brought me home, and drove to Hall's stables, stopping on the way to purchase a new pair of spurs, and a whip, for that was also lost. By the time I mounted the mare it was a quarter past ten, so that I had only three-quarters of an hour to go twelve miles in. I made the noble animal (always willing enough to dash on) put her best leg foremost, and notwithstanding a horrible headache, and at times, sickness, I went at speed the whole distance, the clock striking eleven just as I entered Hampton.

I found the contending parties then in the act of crossing the Thames, having got a volunteer to supply my place as they had given me up. I instantly followed, and thus saved my credit and my money. Our party proved successful, after a hard match. As the Westminsters insisted, we should have won easier had I played as usual; but I was so ill all the time that I let several balls pass me that ought not to have done so, by which our adversaries gained a number of notches. We then adjourned to the Toy [an inn], where a magnificent dinner was prepared, no part of which I could relish, the loss of my money the night before, and the early forfeiture of my promises to my parents, weighing heavily on my spirits. Even champagne failed to cheer me; I could not rally. The moment, therefore, the bill was called for, and our proportions adjusted and paid, I mounted my mare, and in sober sadness gently rode to my father's at Twickenham.

Jim this morning is looking not unlike Hickey must have looked a couple of centuries earlier. I mildly suggest to him that the principal reason might be the same, but he tells me not so, not so. He was running a party disco the night before, and by the time there had been several last dances and all the equipment was packed away it was three in the morning. His stomach aching with emptiness, he decided to fill in with a take-away curry of electric hotness. So that's why he was a bit late getting to the ground this morning. Well, at least we ought to be able to profit by a 'number of notches' as a result of this, because Jim, like William Hickey, plays as a wicket-keeper.

The coin is tossed and a couple of the opposition start padding up, with many a merry quip. Our team and about half of theirs go through the age-old ritual of taking an ancient ball and throwing it around among each other, taking the kind of death-defying catches that somehow always seem to go for four in a match. Sometimes, of course, such balls can be helped on their way by the fielders: many's the time that one of us, in a brave attempt to stop a fast-moving ball with our feet ('Use your bleeding hands!' the rest of the side always shout, forgetting for the moment their own footballing experiences in other matches), has instead given it a kick which has prodded it yet faster over the boundary. One variant of this technique was produced by Norman, our most cowardly fielder, who . . . um, surprise, surprise . . . is not playing for us today. He was bowling in a ten-over beer match and, after he'd sent down about four wides, succeeded at last in getting the ball near enough to the stumps for the batsman to reach it. Like a rocket, it shot straight back towards the bowler, about a foot off the ground. Rather than attempt to catch it or stop it, Norman followed his usual practice of simply doing his best to get out of the way of this hostile projectile. He succeeded with most of his body, but unfortunately left his right ankle behind, and the ball struck it with a sickening splat. 'Well stopped, Norman,' we all cried, applauding soberly as he writhed on the ground, except for one wag who yelled: 'Use your bleeding hands!'

Another variant was produced by Ian Brown of Cheadle Hulme, according to his team-mate Ronnie Locke. In a 1978 match against Marple, Brown had opened the batting and had been dismissed rather cheaply. Depadded, he decided to take a stroll around the boundary with another Cheadle Hulme player, John Howarth (ex Notts, Cheshire and Minor Counties opening bowler), who had yet to bat. It was a pleasant afternoon, and the batsmen were going well: at least one boundary was coming from each over.

The two were ambling along peacably, talking of this and that, when about forty metres ahead of them they saw yet another ball heading swiftly towards the boundary. The grass just beyond the line was particularly long and dense there, and they knew from experience that a ball that went into it could often take a long time to be found again. Accordingly, Brown decided to sprint forward and collect the ball just as it crossed the line and before it could shoot into the long grass. 'Race you to it,' he said to Howarth.

He cut across the outfield and was within a couple of metres of the ball when he heard Howarth directly behind him in hot pursuit. With a happy cackle he gave him a hefty shoulder-charge, sending him sprawling into the undergrowth, and picked up the ball just as it crossed the line. Holding it up in triumph, he turned to where Howarth lay . . . only to find that the white-clad figure lying dazedly in the grass was one of the Marple fielders. Howarth was about thirty metres away, walking towards them with a look of some interest on his face . . .

Our wicket-keeper of the day, Phil, has got his pads and gloves on, and we're throwing the ball in to him – well, in his general direction, that is. This can be a really testing time for a 'keeper: it's all right for the players in professional games, who can prepare to take the ball neatly as it wings in directly over the stumps; but in our team the 'keeper has to be prepared to catch it should it fall anywhere within about a ten-metre radius of the wicket. (Any further away and the rest of the players don't shout: 'Good throw!') Phil is making the most of the practice – leaping this way and that, sometimes dropping his arms to scoop the ball up millimetres from the ground, other times jumping quite astonishing distances into the air to take the ball at full arms-stretch. When you bear in mind that he is fully kitted out with pads, gloves and box, you realize that, despite his bulky figure, he must be something of an athlete. Oh, if only he could pull off this sort of a thing during a game . . .

It's curious that people who can both bat and bowl well are described as all-rounders, whereas wicket-keepers whose batting is good enough that they would anyway qualify for the team are simply called wicket-keepers, or sometimes wicket-keeper/batsmen. Of course, they're really all-rounders, too, because obviously they can't display their versatility by bowling. Some 'keepers take this business of all-round ability to astonishing extremes – for example, 'old Charley Brown, the once Notts wicket-keeper (played for Nottinghamshire, 1843–61)' whom Richard Daft described in his *Cricket Yarns* (1926):

All old cricketers will readily call to mind the wonderful accuracy with which Charley could bowl behind his back, not only straight but with a good length. My friend once saw him play six Englishmen at single-wicket at Calais, the condition being that Charley was allowed to bowl behind his back, and the match ended in an easy victory for him. There is one feat which Charley could accomplish which is so extraordinary that it is scarcely to be credited. It is said that he was able to place an ordinary clay churchwarden pipe on a table in a room, to take part of the stem off, and the pipe to stand on the further side of the room, jerk the piece of the stem of the pipe from behind his back, and with this knock off the small piece which projected from the bottom of the bowl of the churchwarden.

The game has started and Phil the bowler – as opposed to Phil the wicket-keeper – is now running in, his face contorted into as vicious an expression as possible. Facing him is one of the batsmen in flip-flops. If I were Phil, I'd have the irresistible temptation to bowl as fast as possible directly at the fellow's toes – but the chances are that I won't be bowling today; ever since the tendons in my shoulder disintegrated back in May, at the beginning of the season, our captains have been understandably rather unwilling to chance their arm – or, rather, mine – by putting me on to bowl. While fully appreciating and sympathizing with their caution, I nevertheless viciously curse their most intimate intestines as Phil bowls the first ball innocuously short: it bounces a couple of times on its way down the strip and ambles past the batsman, who swipes at it wildly but misses.

No wonder. Behind Phil a helicopter has appeared in the sky, sauntering about from side to side, only a few hundred metres up – if that. It's a smallish craft, painted blue and seeming slightly bluer in the steamy summer haze. It brings the game to a complete standstill. Why? Because it's flying upside-down, that's why. 'I didn't realize that helicopters *could* fly upside-down,' I say to Godfrey, as we all stand looking at this amazing apparition.

'Neither did I,' he says. 'Maybe it's the little green men from Galaxy 49 come to invade us at last. Astonished by the strange terrestrial rite whereby men dress up in white and stand reverentially around on the open grassland, they come to survey the scene and to draw their own alien conclusion about socioreligious practices on this, the third planet from the Sun . . .'

'Nonsense,' I say. 'Extraterrestrials aren't interested in cricket. If they were, the pages of science fiction would be littered with accounts of cricket matches. The only one I can think of off-hand is the one in *Life, the Universe and Everything*. The killer robots. Remember?'

He nods – perchance to sleep.

In Douglas Adams' *Life, the Universe and Everything* (1982), one of his sequels to *The Hitch-Hiker's Guide to the Galaxy*, Arthur Dent and Ford Prefect tumble out of a time-warp to find themselves attending an Australia versus England Test at Lord's just two days before the Earth is to be demolished. For Ford Prefect, who comes from Betelgeuse, the experience is not without some interest – not much, but some: 'I must say, I'm rather fond of cricket, though I wouldn't like anyone outside this planet to hear me saying that. Oh dear no.' For Arthur Dent, though, finding himself at Lord's after his long odyssey through space and time, from the earliest days of mankind on Earth to the last moments of Creation in the Restaurant at the End of the Universe, it is like finding himself back in his mother's embrace. The scene is like that in every cricketer's mind: the scene that is absolutely typical of cricket at its best, although real matches somehow never seem to be quite like that . . .

Outside the refreshment tent, the sun was shining on a happy crowd. It shone on white hats and red faces. It shone on ice lollies and melted them. It shone on the tears of small children whose ice lollies had just melted and fallen off the stick. It shone on the trees, it flashed off whirling cricket bats, it gleamed off the utterly extraordinary object which was parked behind the sight-screens and which nobody appeared to have noticed. It beamed on Ford and Arthur as they emerged blinking from the refreshment tent and surveyed the scene around them.

The match progresses and England win – at the same time retaining the Ashes. As the celebrations proceed and the radio commentators tell the world how frequently the Ashes have been retained in exactly this way and all the other useless, boring statistics with which it has become trendy to regale the listeners, there materializes from nowhere a nebulous spacecraft in the middle of the pitch. From it descend eleven white killer robots carrying what appear to be bats and balls. They start to hit the balls with the bats – but this is cricket with a difference: every time one of the balls lands it explodes with appalling ferocity, killing and maiming spectators and cricketers alike. Ford and Arthur, who fortunately have encountered their old acquaintance Slartibartfast during the proceedings, make their way as swiftly as possible to his spaceship and escape . . . to continue their further and even more harrowing adventures elsewhere. Just to make matters worse, Arthur is told by Slartibartfast, just before they depart, that not only have the killer robots disrupted the game and killed thousands but they've taken the Ashes as well . . .

Much of this is running through my mind – well, lumbering – as I continue to watch the helicopter: will it swing over our pitch, land (how the hell does a helicopter land upside-down?), and disgorge a team of killer robots? Or will the aliens that climb out of it be friendly, interested only in joining in – making it a three-way contest? It's possible, because another science-fiction reference to cricket has just popped into my head. It's from a book which I've never in fact read, but Neil Gaiman has told me about it: *The United Planets* (1962) by Victor Wadey. By the time you read this, you will be able to find the reference in *Ghastly Beyond Belief* (1985), which Neil is compiling with Kim Newman. The plot concerns a planet confusingly named Terra, to distinguish it from Earth. A Terran (*not* an Earth-person – I said this was confusing) has somehow become enamoured of the noblest sport:

The new cricket enthusiast now proceeded to purchase a stock of bats, balls, bails, stumps, gloves and nets, and a great quantity of cricketing manuals to take back to Terra.

'And when I have formed a first class team on Terra,' he announced, 'Terra will challenge the best team that Earth can muster.'

At least Adams has the excuse that he was writing with his tongue firmly in somebody else's cheek: Wadey seems to have been writing quite seriously. Or perhaps, in mocking Wadey, we are really suffering from a failure of the imagination; there is, after all, no logical reason why the members of the Galactic Club should *not* become fascinated by cricket. From our experience here on Earth, we know that some games can cross the cultural barriers with not so much just ease as positive verve: think of the Rubik Cube, which started life behind the Iron Curtain. Think of cricket itself, which is played in some far-flung corners of the world (see pages 120ff) – although the local rules and priorities are not always the same as in the more recognized cricketing nations. There was the time in the Fijian island of Taveuni in 1906, for example, when a match had to be abandoned after only a single ball had been delivered. The ball concerned had, unfortunately, dismissed one of the local chiefs – who was so furious about it that the umpires deemed it wisest not to let the game continue.

Don't laugh at that silly old Fijian chieftain, the primitive. On a much more significant scale, our politicians do much the same sort of thing when they're clean-bowled by a parliamentary question, which shows that they have been lying (sorry, 'misleading the House'). They don't like this game any more, so they stop it.

In the related genre of fantasy, cricket makes its appearance only once, so far as I know – in E. R. Eddison's curious novel *A Fish Dinner in Memison* (1941). The match, however, happens not in some bizarre other-world: all you have to do to find it is to pop through a timewarp. One of the delights of cricket, though, is that you can go quite a long way through a timewarp and still find cricket matches very much like those being played today, differing only in their peripheral details.

Down went another wicket; score, a hundred and fifty-three. 'Now for some fun,' people said as Tom Appleyard came on the field; but Margesson [the incumbent batsman] spoke a wingèd word in his ear: 'Look here, old chap: none of the Jessop business. It's too damned serious now.' 'Ay, ay, sir.' Margesson, in perfect style, sent back the last ball of the over. Appleyard obediently blocked and blocked. But in vain. For one of Bremmerdale's master-creations of innocent outward show and inward guile sneaked round Margesson's defence and took his leg stump. Nine wickets down: total a hundred and fifty-seven: last man, nine. Hyrnbastwick [the opposition], in some elation, were throwing high catches around the field while Dilstead, Anmering's next (and last) man in, walked to the wicket. Margesson said to Tom Appleyard, 'It's up to you now, my lad. Let 'em have it, damn slam and all if you like. But, by Jingo, we must pull it off now. Only seven to win.' Appleyard laughed and rubbed his hands.

There was no more desultory talk: all tense expectancy. 'If Sir Oliver gets the bowling, that puts the lid on it: never hit a ball yet.' 'Why do they play him then?' 'Why, you silly ass, because he's such a thundering good wicket-keeper.' George Cheddisford, about sixteen, home from Winchester because of the measles, maintained a mature self-possession at Lord Anmering's elbow: 'I wish my frater – wish my brother was in again, sir. He'd do the trick.' 'You watch Mr Appleyard: he's a hitter.' By good luck, the ball that had beaten Margesson was the last of the over, so that Appleyard, not Dilstead, faced the bowling: Howard once more, a Polyphemus refreshed. His first ball was a yorker, but Appleyard stopped it. The second, Appleyard, all prudent checks abandoned, stepped out and swiped. Boundary: four. Great applaudings: the parson's children and the two little Rustham boys, with the frenzy of Guelph and Ghibelline, jumped up and down jostling each other. The next ball, a very fierce one, pitched short and rose at the batsman's head. Appleyard smashed it with a terrific overhand stroke: four again – 'Done it!' 'Match!'

Just in case you're feeling like an illiterate thicko because you don't recognize some of the classy references which Eddison used in this account, let me patronizingly pass on to you the results of my frenzied scrabblings in the 1894 edition of *Brewer's Dictionary of Phrase and Fable*:

Polypheme (3 syl.). One of the Cyclops, who lived in Sicily. He was an enormous giant, with only one eye, and that in the middle of his forehead. When Ulysses landed on the island, this monster made him and twelve of his crew captive; six of them he ate, and then Ulysses contrived to blind him, and make good his escape with the rest of the crew. Polypheme was most passionately in love with Galatea, a sea-nymph, but Galatea had set her heart on the shepherd Acis, whom Polypheme, in a fit of jealousy, crushed beneath a rock.

In the gallery of the Farnese palace is a superb painting of

Polyphemus, in three parts; (1) playing a flute to Galatea; (2) hurling a rock at Acis; and (3) pursuing the ships of Ulysses. Poussin has also introduced, in one of his landscapes, Polyphemus sitting on a rock and playing a flute.

So, the next time the opposition have a really fast bowler, you can talk impressively of Polyphemus hurling a rock at Acis. You'll get some funny looks, and you'll probably have to buy your own drinks after the match, but at least you'll have impressed the girls with your erudite classical knowledge. Why not go one better and remember this next?

Guelphs and **Ghibellines**. Two great parties whose conflicts make up the history of Italy and Germany in the twelfth, thirteenth, and fourteenth centuries. Guelph is the Italian form of *Welfe*, and Ghibelline of *Waiblingen*, and the origin of these two words is this: At the battle of Weinsburg, in Suabia (1140), Conrad, Duke of Franconia, rallied his followers with the war-cry *Hie Waiblingen* (his family estate), while Henry the Lion, Duke of Saxony, used the cry of *Hie Welfë* (the family name). The Ghibellines supported in Italy the side of the German emperors; the Guelphs opposed it, and supported the cause of the Pope.

So now you know. Perhaps you wish you didn't.

The upside-down helicopter has by this time departed – and so, for that matter, has the batsman, having edged another shortish delivery to a slip who, to everyone's astonishment, held onto the catch. The new batsman has arrived at the crease, but I'm probably not the only person who's feeling a certain sense of *déjà vu* about all this, because he, too, is clad in shorts and flip-flops. He could easily be the twin brother of his predecessor. Digging a trench for himself, he acknowledges with a grin the various ribald comments thrown at him by Phil the wicket-keeper – 'Every time you bend over, square-leg knows you're not wearing a box,' and the like. He prepares to take his first ball, and successfully negotiates a wide. A few balls later he is not so lucky, and departs towards the pavilion to join his . . . brother? Perhaps they really *are* brothers. If so, there should be no sibling strife this afternoon, because both have recorded exactly the same score.

Intrafamilial warfare – whether the family-members concerned are on the same or opposing sides – is as rife today on the cricket pitch as it ever was during the Civil War. Paul Sylvester has told me of an unusual vendetta which started when he was playing, at the age of 13, for Hendon School. He was captain of the First XI and had scored 93 runs that season for only twice out: he was confidently expecting to finish the season with a healthy average of around – or perhaps even in excess of – 50. However,

The last game of the season was against the Teachers' XI, for whom my father was drafted in at the last moment. The Teachers' XI batted first, made 142, and we had plenty of time to make the runs. I dropped down the order to give some 'youngsters' a chance and also to avoid facing my father, who opened the bowling and took the first three wickets. Anyway, I went in at number 6 to face our rather rotund geography teacher. The second ball I faced was short, outside the off stump, so I stepped across to cut and middled it. Unfortunately the ball went in the general direction of my father at backward square. He took off to his right and held a brilliant catch, so I received my first duck of the season. I cannot put into words my feelings of disgust as I walked back to the pavilion.

Revenge was definitely called for, but the young Paul Sylvester found himself unable suitably to humiliate his father during the succeeding three matches in which the two found themselves playing on opposing sides. Fate

conspired to increase his frustration: on one occasion his
father was palpably out, caught behind off Paul's bowling,
but refused to walk and was given the benefit of the
doubt by the umpire. And then, one day, just as if you'd
read it in *Boys' Own Paper*,

my father played for the parents against the teachers. I went
along to watch, and found that the teachers were one short. My
father came in at number 4 – and he had been having a good
season. I asked one of the maths teachers if I could go close in.
I took up the position of silly mid-off – and, yes, the second ball
I took a one-handed catch to dismiss my father for 0. I had had
to wait six seasons but, you know, it was such a great feeling to
catch him under the same circumstances as he had me . . .

Yes, it's always fun to get your father out, as my daughter
at the age of four implied at the top of her excited voice
the time she got the beach-ball to swing and knocked my
stumps flying. (The wind played a part, I'm sure . . .
irregularities in the pitch . . . bowler's front foot miles
over the crease . . . fly in my eye . . . bat got stuck in the
mud . . .)

And here's Jim, striding out to the crease with a big
grin on his face. He's swinging his bat in the air like a
madman, spinning it as he does so, so that the blade
twinkles in his grasp, dropping it on the grass only the
once and even then partly succeeding in making the
whole thing look deliberate. Having been out first ball
the last time we all saw him play, he's clearly keen to do
something to improve his reputation. Cautiously, despite
the captain's instructions, a few of the out-fielders retreat
a couple of extra yards towards the boundary.

Jim disdainfully lets the first ball go by: it misses his off
stump by a full millimetre. As the bowler runs in for the
second time we can all see that Jim means business this
time: every muscle in his body is tense yet relaxed, and

his eyes are fixed on the round red ball. He's lucky: it's a full toss. His bat moves in a lightning arc, and we all turn our heads in the direction of the square-leg boundary, trying to pick out the ball as it sails in a high trajectory over the fence and in among the cows. All of us, that is, except the bowler and the wicket-keeper, who are looking at Jim's spreadeagled stumps with undisguised pleasure. 'One ball better than last time,' says Phil the wicket-keeper to him with cheery sympathy.

As Jim passes me, head bowed, I hear him muttering about this being the last time – positively the last time – never again – he's had it – hanging up his box for good and all. 'I wouldn't do that,' I say. 'It's nice to have a bit of light relief in our games.' He doesn't even give me the traditional withering glance so beloved by all novelists.

Of course, it's highly unlikely that he really will retire; we all say this sort of gloomy thing the times we're out for next to nothing, or in some other way make fools of ourselves. Of course, professional cricketers really *do* retire from time to time, but at our level of cricket the only form of retirement is the permanent one for which undertakers overcharge.

Not always, though. In Martin Boddey's *The Twelfth Man* (1971) Sir Laurence Olivier recalls his necessarily short cricketing career. He was in his final year at school when his call to glory came: he was in as number 11 to play for his house (or 'set', as a house was called at his school), and thereby was in some small part fulfilling his father's dream that he become a great sportsman.

When it came round to his turn to bat, the situation was tense: seven runs were needed for victory, and he was of course the last man in. Scenes from schoolboy novels crowded through his mind as he strolled confidently – or, at least, he hoped it looked that way – to the wicket. Seven runs for victory: that should be easy enough. Off the remainder of the over he scored two out of the required seven, and in the next over a third run came in the form of a bye, which had the added effect of bringing him down to face the bowling. Only four more runs needed: he could already see himself being chair-lifted to the pavilion, receiving the instant summons to start playing for the first XI . . .

And then he was clean bowled, of course. The irony of it was that the bowler, too, would prove to have a necessarily short cricketing career: his name was Douglas Bader.

Careers can be ended for reasons which have little directly to do with the play of the game on the pitch. Surely the most unusual case of all must be that of poor Gilbert Jessop, 'the Croucher', who played for Gloucestershire and England (and who is therefore really some way outside our scope). In 1916, when he was 42, he was plagued by lumbago, and in hope of a cure allowed himself to be put into a heat-treatment box. Unfortunately, he managed to get himself inextricably trapped in the device, and by the time he was released the heat-treatment had done serious damage to his heart. He was told that, in future, violent exercise of any form was to be avoided. And that was that.

Somehow the Jim Paxton Invitation XI has mustered about 60 runs for the loss of all wickets: not a high score, perhaps, but high enough that the result of the match can't yet be said to be a foregone conclusion. Willy is of course furious that the score has got into double figures, and is telling the tolerantly smiling opposition exactly why they've been so lucky: the umpires were biased, a few batsmen were let off lightly by lousy fielding, our side wasn't at full strength (a favourite line of Willy's, this), the pitch is a sloping one, which always helps the batsmen . . .

Curiously enough, sloping pitches, while they are famous in cricket's popular mythology for allowing mediocre shots to be worth a dozen or more runs, are not always an unalloyed benefit to the batsmen. Bill Pullen tells me of a game he played in the Cotswolds village of Churchill. His partner hit the ball high and hard towards the great vacant space at square-leg, and a six seemed assured. But then, just as the ball was falling contentedly towards the boundary-line, a hand suddenly appeared over the horizon and plucked it out of the air. The fielder responsible had been standing just inside the boundary and, because of the slope of the outfield, had been quite invisible to either batsmen.

Invisible fielders, continues Pullen, were not the only pitfall confronting batsmen who ventured to Churchill. The other was Sid, chairman of the cricket club and a demon umpire who was especially fond of the lbw decision . . . when the opposition was batting. But there was surprisingly little rancour expressed by anybody about this, because Sid had the good sense also to be the local publican, and after the match would dispense free drinks with the same fluency as he had earlier applied to his dubious decisions. Whether the umpiring or the excess of free drinks presented the greater hazard to the visiting batsmen is something we can all debate internally.

In order to shut Willy up, our captain has told him to open the batting – 'That'll hardly give him time to draw breath before he's back here again being boring,' I say, and duck under Willy's whistling bat.

'Will you take the first spell of umpiring, John?' the captain 'asks' me.

'Bloody hell,' says Willy, 'I really won't have a chance

of getting in among the runs if that Marxist poofter psychopath is umpiring. He'd have me up against a firing-squad as soon as look at me.'

'Most people would rather have you up against a firing-squad than look at you,' I say to him courteously. 'Just remember, *mein Führer*, that the umpire's decision is final.'

'Pinko bearded fifth columnist, onanist and pederast,' counters Willy with all the wit and subtlety at his command.

'Ah, shuddup and go back to the *Daily Telegraph*.'

'Ken Livingstone ought to be strung up by the goolies.'

'At least he's got some.'

'Glad I'm not a newt. Have to spend all the time with my back to the wall.'

'Just be thankful umpiring isn't democratic. If I put it to the vote you'd be out before you got to the crease. By the way, I think I owe you a pint.'

'You do, you Trot bastard.'

And so we wend our happy way out to the centre, Willy pausing from time to time to tell members of the fielding side that they're enemies within, terrorist moles dedicated to bringing the Free World under the yoke of the Soviets, and so on. I confirm to the bowler that yes, indeed, Willy really is always like this, and then take great pleasure in giving my friend his guard: 'A bit to the left . . . a bit further to the left . . . no, you're still too far right . . .'

I don't even have to lift my finger, a few seconds later, when Willy's stumps are flattened. And there was I all ready to accept an appeal for caught behind.

'Messrs Wintergreen will be thinking they're throwing their sponsorship money away,' says the wicket-keeper, fanning a hand as Willy departs.

'He's old,' I say. 'He has to put that stuff on in case his muscles seize up completely.'

'Stalinist nancy. I wouldn't drink your pint if it killed me,' Willy hurls back over his shoulder, before vanishing behind a mist of anti-socialist slogans.

Sponsorship, even at fairly low levels of cricket, is now so rife that one wonders where the game itself ends and its commercial aspects begin. Sooner or later one of those appealing little dogs that run onto the pitch during important Test matches is going to be seen dragging a toilet roll behind it. In fact, sponsorship is far from new: the first English touring team to visit Australia, way back in the last century, was sponsored by the company Spiers & Pond. It's perhaps rather galling to realize that Spiers & Pond forked out the cash for the cricketers only because they'd been unable to set up their first preference, a lecture tour by Charles Dickens. Hadn't the men of Mammon got their cultural priorities a bit mixed up?

'Sponsorship' is perhaps not quite the right word to use for the Church of England's relationship with the game, but somewhere in the English language there must be a word very much like it to apply to the situation. In order to get some guidance on the matter I wrote to John Trevisick, who very kindly supplied me with a long description of the Church's activities in this area. Of course, far be it from me to suggest that the respected gentlemen of the cloth actually plumb the bottom-most depths of cricket like their lay fellows, but . . .

One of the best cricket stories which has gone the rounds and lost nothing in the telling concerns a Church of England parson whose bishop considered he should move from one parish to another.

In duty bound the clergyman, who was young, considered it prudent to cast a critical eye on the church, the vicarage and its amenities, not least the garden. In due course, his nonacceptance of the offer was couched in a diplomatically phrased letter to the bishop who, to his dying day, was in blissful ignorance concerning the real reason. The lawn would not accommodate a full-length cricket pitch complete with nets. The priest has since enjoyed the best of both worlds, and is still playing competitive cricket – a tower of strength in keeping the flag flying.

Organized cricket for clergymen of the Church of England and the Church in Wales predates Gillette, Benson and Hedges and the John Player sponsored competitions, and, after over thirty years, it still retains its popularity.

The origin merits repetition. In the immediate postwar years a few priests who served smallish communities (Wantage, Abingdon and Lambourn excepted) on the Berkshire Downs had encountered one another in corporate religious observances such as patronal festivals (special services held in connection with, for instance, a local church dedicated to St Augustine or St Mary), and perhaps an alfresco meal to follow in the vicarage garden – an occasional cricket match, too.

To the writer's knowledge there existed what in later days became known as a 'Gang of Four', who came together with other clerics in friendly matches, and they hatched up the notion that it might be possible to create a national competition for Anglican clergymen. They came to the office of the *Church Times* in London and put up the idea to the then proprietor, Mr Christopher Palmer, head of the family which has owned and produced the paper for well over a century. One of the delegation happened to be the son of one of Mr Christopher's personal friends.

He threw this particular hot potato in the direction of his News Editor [i.e., Trevisick] to discover whether an open competition would be feasible, and particularly to ascertain the measure of support which would be forthcoming. It was also made clear that the possible organization of such a venture would be a voluntary labour of love!

Soundings were taken and the upshot was an astonishingly large measure of support, but there were traps for the unwary. A knock-out 'sudden death' system involving long-distance travel was abandoned and in its place came the formation of regions and sub-regions designed to cover all parts of England and Wales. In late 1982 the groupings were:

Region 1A: Blackburn, Carlisle, Liverpool, Manchester, Sheffield, Chester

Region 1B: Bradford, Durham, Newcastle, Ripon, Wakefield, York

Region 2A: Birmingham, Hereford, Lichfield, Oxford

Region 2B: Ely, Norwich, Peterborough, Southwell

Region 3A: Chelmsford, London, St Albans, Southwark

Region 3B: Canterbury, Chichester, Guildford, Rochester

Region 4A: Llanduff, Monmouth, St Davids, Swansea and Brecon

Region 4B: Bath and Wells, Bristol, Gloucester, Worcester

This shows that the only English absentees in 1982 were Winchester, Bristol, Coventry, Derby, Exeter, Leicester, Lincoln, Portsmouth, St Edmundsbury and Ipswich, Salisbury, Truro, and Sodor and Man (the Isle of Man). The Welsh absentees were Bangor and St Asaph.

Truro and Sodor and Man would find it hard to raise a team, as numbers of ordained men are smaller than in other dioceses; moreover, travelling puts participation out of the question. The two Welsh dioceses not included lie in the northern half of the Principality, and they have kindred problems. In times of high-cost petrol, car-sharing – where possible – is the order of the day and venues for matches are, invariably, equidistant between the opposing sides. It is to the credit of the clergy, who are certainly not overpaid, that they bend over backwards to share the economic load involved in competitive cricket.

Liverpool have been in the final on fourteen occasions (including every year since 1969) and won the championship on six of these. Sheffield have also made their way to the top six times. St Davids are the only Welsh team to add a plinth on the trophy by virtue of an abandoned match; Llandaff were on the losing side twice in the first three years.

Two of the St Davids players have since been elevated. George Noakes has been elected Bishop of St Davids and Lawrence Bowen is Dean of St Davids Cathedral. Both were on view when they welcomed the Queen and the Duke of Edinburgh to the Royal Maundy Observance in early 1982, thus enabling old friends to see them perform on a different wicket.

Wales's former primate, the late Dr John Morgan, graced a semifinal in which his own diocese, Llandaff, was playing in Reading, in the early days. He broke a journey to see how things were progressing, leaving with the admonition: 'If you don't win, don't bother to come back!' His successor, Dr Morris, went one better by playing for his diocese (Monmouth). Eight other bishops have turned out for their dioceses. One, who assumed the captaincy, was noted for his unepiscopal comments at the drop not of a hat but of a catch.

No priest, either on ordination or on arrival from another diocese, should be surprised if he is met at his first interview with his bishop with the enquiry: 'Do you play cricket?' Our fathers in God generally get their priorities in the right order.

Bishop David Sheppard is seen these days, not in white flannels but in a lounge-suit cheering his side on, and photographers make a beeline towards him as he obliges the young sons of parson-cricketers, who turn an arm and bowl to him on the sidelines. He rarely misses a final when Liverpool is participating.

The final match has always been played on the historic Walker ground at Southgate in North London. It has attracted among its distinguished guests Sir Pelham Warner and Mr C. B. Fry; among its staunchest supporters was Sir Hubert Ashton, a former president of Essex and the MCC who captained Cambridge. Mr E. W. Swanton graced an inter-round game between Southwark and Chichester at the Oval and renewed links with cricketers he had encountered in his own playing days.

When writing about clerical cricket one cannot but refer to the contribution which ordained clergymen of the Church of England have made to the summer game in the long ago. One has read how the Rev. W. Rashleigh (Essex and Kent) knocked up 160 before lunch. There were two remarkable parsons christened Charles – Charles Ward and Charles Studd. Before them John Mitford and James Pycroft were of note, the latter finding time to write authoritatively on the summer game. It was claimed that at one period Leicestershire could call upon seven clergymen – funerals permitting, presumably!

Also predating the *Church Times* Cup competition, a mighty contribution was made by Canon Jack Parsons, a contemporary of R. E. S. Wyatt. Canon F. H. Gillingham played for Essex, and his son Peter, when Vicar of Horsham, was an outstanding participant in the *Church Times* Cup. So was Canon W. E. G. Payton, CB, who had also played in county cricket. E. T. Killick, Middlesex and England, was another great clerical cricketer, and P. D. S. Blake, remembered for his brilliance as a player at Eton and Oxford and now a country parson on the Kent–Sussex border, still turns out for Chichester.

I'm now back in the pavilion listening to the distinctly non-clerical language being used by our team to describe their various batting failures – and in fact the situation really is a tight one: seven runs to get and only four wickets standing. One of those wickets is mine, so I find a tatty pair of pads floating around and put them on. Mitch is still out there, batting determinedly; he's playing one of his more introverted innings, in which the aim seems to be not so much to win the match but to make damn' sure that half the opposition die of old age before it's over, and so don't have any of the satisfaction of victory.

There's a cheer from the opposition and Phil the wicket-keeper appears in front of us, cursing at the bat, the ground, us, his gloves, his pads, his boots and various intimate parts of the umpires. 'It's my bloody hands,' he says in one of his politer moments. 'They're so bloody sore from all you bloody lot throwing the ball in at me.'

'I didn't know any of this other lot could throw it in hard enough to hurt even your lily-white hands, you red pansy,' says Willy.

'At least,' says Phil wearily, 'oh He Who Must Be Abused, they can stop the ball in the first place, so as to be able to throw it in.'

'You should put steak in your gloves,' says Vince.

'Steak! I couldn't afford to put soyaburger in them,' says Phil, but not in time to stop someone from telling the tale of Tommy Birtles.

Tommy Birtles, you see, was a Barnsley player. On the morning of the first of three one-day matches, Birtles and the Barnsley wicket-keeper were on their way to the ground when the latter made a swift detour into the butcher's shop to buy some steak to go inside his gloves. However, because of a sudden deluge of rain, the match was abandoned even before it started, and so the wicket-keeper, a bachelor, generously gave Birtles the steak to take home for his family's supper.

On the second of the three days, exactly the same thing happened: free steak for the Birtles family. On the third morning, however, just as the 'keeper was about to go into the butcher's, Birtles stopped him and, looking up at the ominous clouds gathering in the greying sky, said flatly: 'Better get chops. We're tired of steak.'

And that is the Tommy Birtles story. By the time it's been told, we need only three runs to win and there are still two wickets standing. I'm the next man in, which is so exciting that, under the circumstances, I have to nip round to the back of the pavilion to use the lavatory yet again. After an extremely painful struggle with my box, I return to find that a wide has put us within one run of the visitors' total. Surely even *we* – even the West Country Publishers' Cricket Club – can't foul this one up?

Simon Raven writes of a similarly tight finish in his cricketing autobiography, *Shadows on the Grass* (1982). In the summer of 1957 he was batting in an army match: seven runs were required for victory, and there would be time for one more over if the one now in progress finished before the magic hour of 6·30. There were three minutes still to go, and the bowler was running in to complete the final over when a telegram boy walked onto the pitch and straight up to Raven.

Raven took the telegram and waved the boy away – but the boy refused to go. 'Might be a reply,' he insisted firmly.

'No reply,' said Raven.

But, said the boy, how did Raven know this if he hadn't opened the telegram? No, he wouldn't go and stand over by the pavilion for a few minutes; he wasn't going to hang around all night, now was he? Eventually Raven ripped the blasted thing open to read:

PLEASE PAY ONE HUNDRED SEVENTY OWING MONDAY LATEST OR COMPELLED TO INFORM COMMANDANT BEST RESPECTS THEWS JAMESON TURF ACCNT

But the wind seized the telegram from Raven's gloved grasp, and it blew cheekily across the grass, with Raven close behind it, to be fielded by the commandant, who gestured that he would look after it until the close of the match. Miserably, the clock having struck 6·30, Raven watched as his batting partner hit what was now the last ball of the game for a courageous six – especially miserably, because this tied the scores and he'd bet £25 against the match ending in a draw.

'My only consolation,' wrote Raven, 'was that the Commandant had been too much of a gentleman to read my telegram before giving it back to me.'

As it proves, however, *we're* not going to be subjected to the ignominy of a draw – or, just as bad, a defeat – for Mitch and Rudolph between them scrape the final few runs. As happens so often, I'm in the twittish position of having to take off all my various bits of armour without even having had to stroll out to the centre, let alone face a ball. The only advantage of this is that, by the time you've got rid of your pads, etc., most of the other players are at the bar ordering drinks, but haven't yet had long enough to complete buying the first round: if you play your cards right you can time it precisely so that . . .

'Why, yes, Willy,' I say. 'I'll have a pint, please. That makes it two I owe you. By the way, can I hitch a lift back into town?'

'No,' he says.

'I'll say I'm a Marxist poofter.'

'No, it's not that. It's just I don't have my car with me today. Why don't you ask one of those commie sympathizers Jim brought along to take you back to Exeter?'

And so, sure enough, I end the evening having a long chat about this, that and the other (inevitably, quite a lot of the other) with a couple of people who're heading back my way. This is one of the great charms of cricket, for me. In the ordinary course of events I would probably never have met these people, and yet here I am enjoying their company. (They're probably bored silly with mine, but that's beside the point.)

John Trevisick mentioned the fact of car-sharing in his discussion of clerical cricket, and in fact car-sharing plays a pretty important part with most teams – certainly in the West Country, where the distances players have to cover can be pretty long, and where some people, like me, just don't drive. This was the case even more so in the time of our parents, and of our parents' parents, when often it was a matter less of car-sharing than of cart-sharing. In his *Happy Days* (1933) James Thorpe recounts with delight the experience which he gave to some unfortunate cricketer during the 1914 season:

To one of our matches I took an unsuspecting fellow-cricketer in the sidecar of an old motor cycle I had recently bought. It was my first and last connection with these infernal machines. With a vigorous push-off by the mechanic at the garage we started gaily, and with the oppressive consciousness of my ignorance I hoped for the best. At one corner, which I took too closely, we mounted a high bank, hovered perilously on the top, and fortunately slid back on to the road, nearly colliding with a peaceful lady on a push-bike who failed to understand our unusual manoeuvres. Continuing our wild career we rushed three water-splashes at full speed. I was fortunately protected by overalls, but my passenger in a thin flannel suit was swamped. We eventually arrived around an hour and a half late. He was soaked to the skin, and the inside of my knees was scorched by an almost white-hot engine. An expert explained that we had done the fourteen miles in the lowest gear and that it was a miracle that our engine had not seized up. Before the return journey I had some useful practical instruction, and it says much for the pluck of my passenger that he insisted on accompanying me back.

Oddly enough, I had a vaguely parallel experience while purchasing the only motorbike I've ever owned – 'my first and last connection with these infernal machines'. The garage-hand who was selling it to me patiently explained what I should do to start it, change gear, rev up the throttle and so on. It was only when I was cruising merrily along a back road at 30mph that I realized that he had omitted to tell me how to slow down and stop the bloody thing . . .

Tonight, though, there's no question of a motorbike or sidecar. The person who's so kindly giving me a lift has a newish-looking four-door, so all is well. Jim has recovered miraculously from his late-night curry, and is swapping jokes with the others just before stripping off to do a few miles' road-running (the masochist). About half of the rest of the cricketers have already peeled off for home. The night is coming in, and it's been one of those afternoons where the weather has been such that you abruptly begin to feel profoundly sleepy about an hour after you stop running around. I'm only too pleased when my new friend suggests that we make a move.

We've had a scratch match, nothing more – but at the same time we've all had a lot of fun. One can't really envisage our more professional brothers being able to say to each other: 'Come on, we've got a pitch booked for

Sunday and no one to play against. See if you can rustle up a team.' Even if they did go in for this sort of a thing, you can't really see them *enjoying* it.

It would be nice to open the bowling at Lord's – just once. After that first time it might well start to become just a trifle tedious.

Or maybe not.

6
THE BARBECUE MATCH
25th August, 1984

'You bastard!' hisses my wife to me as the 'bus lurches out of Exeter on its way towards Newton Abbot.

I, who have been looking forward to the weekend, grinning inanely out of the window at the sunlit streets, turn to look at her in some astonishment. 'Have I done something wrong?'

'Yes, you clown. You told the driver we were only going to be away for one night.'

'But we *are* going to be away for only the one night. He wanted to know if we were coming back tomorrow so that he could sell us cheap return tickets.'

'You could have paid the extra.'

'What the hell are you talking about, darling?'

'Even if you wanted to save a few bob, you needn't have told him in such a loud voice. Now everyone on the 'bus will know.'

'But why shouldn't they know? It's not as if I passed round copies of our address and told burglars to try the bog window.'

'Well, just look at it.' She points at our camping gear, most of which we have crammed with difficulty into the luggage section at the front of the 'bus. The kettle and the pan, which I've tied to the outside of my rucksack in the way I used to do, twenty years ago, as a Boy Scout, clang merrily together. The professional image is somewhat spoilt by the rear half of Jennifer Dog, my daughter's favourite stuffed toy, sticking out of one of the other rucksacks.

'Um, yes, I see what you mean,' I say. 'It does look

like rather a lot of luggage for twenty-four hours. Perhaps you ought to have left the tumble-drier behind.' I take the kick stoically: I'm British after all.

But, yes, it's true. The Grants have at last taken the plunge and invested in some camping gear – and this is the very weekend when it's going to undergo its field-testing . . . literally. This afternoon we're going to play the Quakkers, a team of doctors and assorted medicos from Plymouth, and after the match there's going to be the highlight of the West Country Publishers' CC calendar, the annual barbecue. Public transport in this part of the world having been made more efficient (i.e., slashed to the extent that it now has about the same status in most people's minds as the hippogryph), we've had to face the stark choice of missing the beano and all its attendant boozing or camping overnight near to the cricket ground: the latter is obviously the preferable choice. For me, it has the added advantage that my wife will be there with me, ready to stop me from any indiscretions such as an earnestly drunken attempt to chat up the heavy roller. So here we are, travelling light, ready to breathe the fresh countryside air and fill ourselves with radiant health in all directions – barely able to walk under the weight of our camping kit, it's true, but then even that is part of the great tradition of enjoying oneself in the cathedral of the outdoors. Camping is rather like Texan boots: they're worth wearing because of the blessed feeling of comfort that flows through you when you take the damned things off. Thanks to all the little extras that might come in useful over the weekend, this is, by the same principle, going to be one of the best short holidays of our lives.

I try to change the subject. 'Did you know that they used to have cricket matches in China, too?' I ask.

'So what.'

'Yes,' I say, warming to the theme, 'only they were rather different from the ones we have now . . .'

'*You* have now.'

'. . . because the Chinese used actual crickets – you know, the things like grasshoppers. They used to set them against each other, on the same sort of basis as cock-fighting.' My wife isn't interested, so I turn to my daughter and continue. 'What was really interesting, Jane, is the way they used to feed them.'

'Not Weetabix?'

'No, not Weetabix. You see, crickets eat insects, so what the owners used to do, in order to make their champions big and strong, was to encourage mosquitoes to sit on their arms and suck blood out of their veins and arteries. Then, when the mosquitoes were all bloated with the blood and, so the people thought, filled with all the owners' strength, they were fed to the crickets.'

Jane taps my wife on the shoulder. 'Mummy, Daddy's being disgusting again.'

'I bet you didn't know that a mosquito can fly carrying twice its own weight of blood,' I say limply, before my wife's stare withers me completely.

'Tone it down a bit,' she says. 'You'll give the little rat nightmares. Where do you get all this junk from, anyway?'

'Oh, here and there,' I say modestly. 'I was reading only the other day about an Australian cricketer during the Bodyline tour of 1932/3 who got himself a new dog and called it "Larwood". And nobody could understand why he gave it the name until he explained to them that it was because the dog had four short legs and its balls swung both ways . . .' I giggle. Catherine doesn't. Jane doesn't. It's possible that neither of them has ever heard of Harold Larwood. Probably the tale's apocryphal, anyway, and, come to think of it, it's not actually all that funny, either. Oh God.

Conversation is at best sporadic for the rest of the journey to Newton Abbot. Flexing our shoulders like the wide-open-spaces types in Marlboro Country preparing to heft their iron lungs, we climb with some difficulty off the 'bus, our rucksacks tangling and jamming in the too-narrow doorway. I stand on the concrete of what I believe is an award-winning 'bus-station – the prestigious Auschwitz Medal, no doubt – and remark: 'It's great to be back in the country.'

'Don't worry,' says Catherine, 'I still love you anyway.'

Paranoia leaps unrestrained in my bosom: why did she have to *say* that, just now? A gesture is called for.

'I know it's expensive,' I mumble, 'but I think I've got just about enough cash for us to get a taxi to the campsite. Come on.' So we rush to the taxi-rank, while I console myself with the thought that what we're doing is really just the same as hitch-hiking, which is professionally respectable in camping circles, only we're paying the driver.

Soon we're almost there, passing the 'Two Mile Oak' on the right. 'Handy for the pub,' I say cheerfully, receiving a sullen grunt in return. 'We'll have to go in there for a drink at some point,' I say. 'It was the landlord who helped me on the 'phone the other day to track down the campsite.'

Campsites have changed since the days of my youth. For a start, they're all packed with caravans, some of which are quite obviously permanent fixtures, since they lack wheels, and all of which sprout television aerials. We don't even have a transistor radio with us, and so will be forced to play charades, or something. The pitch we're directed to is conveniently close to the lavatories/showers complex, built in sensible, efficient concrete and plastered with notices saying NO SMOKING; when I was a lad it was a hole in the ground, and you *had* to smoke to keep the flies off. 'Those were the days when men were men,' I remark to Catherine.

'Well, you can show that they still are by pitching the tent,' she says.

Putting up the tent takes only a few minutes for an old pro like me, and soon I'm gazing proudly at it. The campsite-owner joins me, and likewise looks at it admiringly for a moment before pointing out to me that one of my guy-ropes stretches across an invisible pathway that separates our pitch from the next. Could I possibly move the tent? – 'not far: just a couple of feet'. An hour or so later, after I've attempted several different ways of making the necessary change without having to strike the tent completely, and after I've damaged the flysheet, all is shipshape again. Unfortunately, because of the palaver, we have no time to cook lunch on our spanking-new gas stove, and so we stick a pork pie in the kid's hand and set off in our different directions: Catherine and Jane for a country ramble (they'll join me at the match at teatime) and me for a quick one in the 'Two Mile Oak' before going on to the ground.

Pubs and cricket have been associated almost since the start of the game, all those years ago. On good days the pub does rapid business before, during and after the match, with sorrows being drowned and victories being celebrated; on bad days, in the times before licensing laws, the pub was a haven from the elements, with the would-be cricketers consoling themselves with an extended session of their second-favourite sport. I've often wondered why games which start late because of rain are described as 'weather-affected', when everyone knows that really they should be called 'beer-affected'. Sometimes the games can start so late that, in effect, they never actually start at all. I don't mean the matches where there is no play, and both teams go home crediting themselves with a draw. No, in some games in some parts of the world no one will go home until there is a positive, definite result. Our ancestors, upon whose matches very large sums of money often rested, in the form of bets, simply let a game of cricket continue over however many days were necessary – a practice which must have caused havoc among the lives of some of the players, who were expected to return to their jobs. At some more recent time – and I've got no idea when – an alternative system was introduced whereby each member of each team has to bowl at the undefended stumps, the team which hits the wickets most times out of their eleven balls being declared the winner. When such sudden-death 'matches' are additionally beer-affected, of course, they can last almost as long as a full cricket match. Perhaps this explains why in Kent on one occasion the result had to wait until the last ball bowled by the last player of the second team, who gave his side a 1–0 victory. Much longer, though, was a contest between Rossie Priory and Fochabers, in Scotland in 1979, where the score after 22 balls was tied at 2–2, and the teams eventually had to bowl three times each before Rossie Priory carried the day by 9–6.

Beer seems to play its part in the annual match between the press and the TUC General Council. According to Keith Harper, Labour Editor of the *Guardian* and captain of the journalists' side (in a letter to me dated 17th November, 1982), this fixture has been in existence since 1963 'or thereabouts'. That the spirit of true low-level cricketing sportsmanship plays a major role in these encounters can be gathered from Alan Rusbridger's *Guardian* report of the 1982 fixture:

The truth can now be told about the TUC General Council's so-called 'victory' in their annual so-called cricket match against the gentlemen of the press. This hallowed contest takes place each year in the grounds of what was the print union NATSOPA's rest home at Rottingdean.

This year the grand old men of The Movement scored rather more than 100, largely due to the scorer, Miss Ada Maddocks (NALGO), who is of the fixed opinion that each time a General Council batsman touches the ball, he has made four runs.

The less grand old men of the Noblest Profession were replying briskly – indeed, impartial observers believe they had already passed their opponents' score – when an alert fielder, Mr Ken Gill (AUEW-TASS), noticed that the SOGAT '82 beer tent had opened. The field followed Mr Gill's example. So did the batsmen. The game was awarded, on the Maddocks principle, to the Brothers.

But, thanks to Rusbridger, the press got the last word.

Bill Pullen of Gotherington CC tells of an away game against Llanelli Wanderers. Fred Mac – Pullen tactfully gives him only this name – was the star of the Gotherington bowling: it was largely as a result of his fine efforts, as well as some fine work in the field by the rest of the team, that the Llanelli side was dismissed for a mere 57. As the players came in off the field, Fred Mac was told by his skipper to prepare himself to go in to bat at number four.

Since the total needed by Gotherington was a reasonably small one – to put it kindly – Fred Mac saw little reason not to adjourn to the bar in the pavilion and celebrate his doughty bowling feats by the time-honoured method of sinking a pint or three. In fact, however, as things turned out he was to his surprise required to bat – although by the time he found his way unsteadily to the wicket there were only four more runs needed for victory. He responded to the situation with all the instinctive batting grace of the born bowler: he did his best to hit the first straight ball to come his way into the Irish Sea. There was the romantic sound of leather cracking against wood – but unfortunately the wood in question was his wicket.

He didn't seem too concerned, but made his way happily back to the pavilion. 'What happened, then, Fred?' asked his team-mates as he struggled with the straps on his pads.

''S easy,' came the carefully enunciated reply. 'I just . . . saw three balls, 'n' picked the wrong bugger to hit.'

In the days when pubs were very closely associated indeed with local cricket clubs – the landlords often owned the pitches, ran the clubs, sold cricketing equipment, etc., etc. – and were, in addition, open at any hours the landlord wanted them to be, such events cannot have been uncommon. Indeed, if you've ever wondered while poring over old cricketing records why so many cricketers were called Lushington, and never seemed to score many runs, the answer is at hand: it was because the word 'lushington' was the slang for a drunkard (we still have the word 'lush'), and the appearance of the name in the scorebook simply indicated that some poor inebriate, incapable even of pronouncing his name clearly, had been dragged out of the pub to make up the numbers.

Such things are only to be expected at our level of cricket – although, since the earliest days, some clubs have seen fit to introduce a system of fines and forfeited wickets to deter their recognized players from turning up at matches in a drunken state. (Ours would be a much richer club if we had this sort of rule.) At the rather elevated levels, though, the crime is obviously a far more serious one – and the penalties for committing it are correspondingly much harsher. A professional cricketer called Bobby Peel, of Yorkshire, actually put an end to his first-class cricketing career through being guilty of drunkenness at a match – although perhaps he did go a little over the top: he staggered with difficulty onto the pitch, opened his flies, and ostentatiously urinated in front of his captain, Lord Hawke.

As I've said, local pubs could do such good business on the day of a cricket match – selling food and drink not only to the players but also to the often quite large crowds of spectators who gathered to watch even relatively lowly matches – that their landlords found it worthwhile to encourage the sport in every possible way, by providing the pitch, acting as groundsmen, allowing the pub to be used for club meetings and displaying the names of the sides picked for forthcoming matches. The classic example is of course that of the Bat and Ball Inn at Hambledon, but there were countless other pubs and landlords whose association with cricket was every bit as intimate. In his excellent *Cricket: A Social History 1700–1835* (1972) John Ford gives the names of a number of pubs named after the sport, from the obvious ones like 'The Cricketers' Arms' onward, and confesses that his 'own particular favourite is The Sign of the Hit or Miss in Chatham, which was so named by 1787'.

An extension of the pub/cricket principle of the eighteenth and nineteenth centuries was the granting to publicans of franchises to erect booths around the ground on the day of a cricket match. In some cases these were jealously guarded, exclusive and expensive monopolies; in others you might find a goodly number of beer tents to choose from – to the extent that, in 1834 in Nottingham, a cricketer called Clarke challenged a full eleven of the publicans represented at the ground to a single-wicket match. Whether the drink was bought from booths or from the nearby tavern, there can be no doubt that there was a good deal of slurred frivolity at these matches – although, as we shall see, when women tried to import similar intoxication into their matches, their menfolk were less than amused.

Possibly the most important example of the pub/cricket interaction, however, concerns the Star and Garter in Pall Mall and the formation of one of Britain's best-known institutions. In fact, the Star and Garter had had a long history of involvement with the greatest of sports, because it was at a meeting in the inn of the Society of Noblemen and Gentlemen in 1744 that the Articles of the Game of Cricket were hammered out and finalized; and at a similar meeting at the Star and Garter in 1774 important revisions were made. But it was in 1787 that possibly the most significant meeting took place at the pub: members of the White Conduit Club met and decided that henceforth their club should be the Marylebone Cricket Club.

Nowadays, however, pubs have been reduced from such important positions – at least in terms of the first-class game – and instead must be satisfied with the absolutely crucial role they play in the lower-level game. Of course, there are still today plenty of pubs which field their own teams, following in the footsteps of a tradition that goes back more than two centuries. The pub teams of today are, in general, great fun to play – as soon as you've recognized Grant's Second Law. This states that the chap in the blue jeans, coloured shirt and street-shoes, who when chucking the ball around beforehand looks like the team buffoon, is in fact an excellent, accurate bowler who can move it both ways, and, when batting, has such a keen eye and powerful shoulders that he's capable of snicking sixes through the slips – literally through, if need be. (Grant's First Law, better known as Grant's Improbability Law, is concerned with the paranormal, and so need not detain us here.)

But of all the associations between beer and cricket,

there can surely be none closer than that involved in an annual match played between two teams from Lincoln College, Oxford, where the beer has actually been written into the local rules. At this match, between the Davenant Society and the Lollards, all the players concerned must have a pint beer-mug with them at all times; these mugs are refilled when necessary by a couple of co-opted freshers. The beer is used as the basic medium, as it were, for the penalties which are imposed during the game by the umpires. For example, when a batsman somehow manages to get his score into double figures, he must down a statutory pint, and every five further runs he scores involve the draining of a further half-pint; the offence is officially described as Gross Competence. Pushing along to much higher scores is, however, a pretty difficult business, because there is a further penalty of a pint for hitting a four (except an accidental one); and the whole situation is exacerbated yet further for the side which is batting second, because by that time they will already have been somewhat debilitated by the various penalties imposed upon them for playing such dirty tricks as bowling somebody out, stumping someone, taking a catch, and so forth. A further hindrance to high scoring is that the umpires may respond to appeals not only from the fielding side but also from those members of the batting side who feel that it's getting to be time when *they* had a knock.

In fact, it must be an advantage for the umpires, if no one else, to stay sober at least until after the match, because there are various other tricksy rules with which they have to cope, like the one which states that they must ensure that the game ends in a draw. Even more complicated to master is the 'dead ants' rule. This comes into play when, for example, the batsman has skied the ball and it looks as if there might be a catch in the offing.

The umpires must, at exactly the right moment, shout 'Dead ants!', and the players must respond by throwing themselves on their backs and waving their arms and legs in the air. As in the children's game of musical statues, there is a penalty for being the last player to obey the instruction: he's got to drink yet another pint of beer.

In light of these connections between cricket and booze, it is hardly surprising to find in the records of the eighteenth- and nineteenth-century clubs that rather more attention was often paid to the booze than to the game itself. Here for example is a longish extract from the *Annals of the Teignbridge Cricket Club* (1888), in which the book's compiler, G. Wareing Ormerod, shows clearly that he has his priorities right, and that the same was true of the worthies involved in setting up the club:

It was soon evident that Cricket was not to be the only subject of the Club. On the 24th June, 1824, ten ladies and twenty-four gentlemen came to the meeting as visitors, and that their reception was satisfactory may be judged from the fact, that on the following 1st and 29th of July, and 7th of August, similar compliments were paid to the Club. The first 'Ladies' Day' was on June 23rd, 1825, when twenty-five ladies and twenty-two gentlemen came as visitors, and since that time those happy meetings have been continued to the present day. Each member could for several years invite an unlimited number of friends, but the meetings became so much liked that it was found needful to limit the number of invitations. Changes as to the manner of issuing invitations, and as to the number of visitors that each member may invite, have been made from time to time, each change giving proof that after the passing of more than sixty years there is the same wish, as in olden days, to be present at 'Teignbridge Ladies' Days.' The records do not say whether dancing took place at the first of these meetings, but it is evident that this soon was the case, and also that these pleasant meetings were reserved for the days on which special matches took place, and the Decennial Jubilees.

For a long time the dancing took place upon the grass. At the first jubilee, on August 1st, 1833, dancing commenced 'under the canopy of Heaven,' and was continued in the tent and room 'until the midnight hour.' There were present as visitors 180 ladies and 141 gentlemen, and 50 members. On a Ladies' Day, June 20th, 1839, there was a heavy thunderstorm, and a band was sent for from Teignmouth, and the dance was by candlelight in the room. On July 18th, in the same year, it rained, and 'the ladies were obliged to dance in the house.' To remedy this a marquee was purchased; but on August 18th, 1840, it blew so hard that the marquee could not be put up, and it rained so heavily after dinner that the tables were cleared in the dining-room, and dancing was kept up there with spirit until after eight o'clock. From entries in 1844 it appears that dancing 'was kept up until nightfall,' but it is evident that, except on special occasions, the ladies left at an early hour. Their comfort was not, however, neglected; as on July 10th, 1845, the Secretary was instructed to expend £20 on a new floor for the dining-room before the next Ladies' Day. From time to time improvements have taken place until a complete change has been made, the Pavilion having become the dancing-room, and the marquee the place for refreshments during the dances. In the years 1850, 1852, and 1853 Ladies' Tea Parties were given. On June 27th, 1866, it was resolved that on Ladies' Days no dance should be commenced after 11·45 P.M., and that 'God Save the Queen' should be played punctually at 11·45. A further change was made in 1888, directing that on Ladies' Days dinner should take place at 3·30 P.M., that dancing should commence at six, and 'God Save the Queen' be played punctually at eleven.

There, now we know all the important details of the setting-up and early history of Teignbridge CC. Oh, hang on a minute, there was something else, I'm sure. It's on the tip of my . . . Ah, yes:

As regards Cricket, at the commencement of the Club every member who was not on the ground at eleven o'clock was to be fined two shillings and sixpence [a lot in those days], and those who did not attend the Meeting, five shillings. These fines were soon done away with. On May 26th, 1825, it was resolved that wickets should be pitched at half-past ten, and that a bell should be bought to give notice as to dinner and resumption of play.

'By-days' frequently took place on the Thursdays between the
regular days of meeting, and then the losing side had to pay for
the dinner. On March 23rd, 1844, it was determined that regular
meetings should take place once a fortnight in June, and on
every Thursday in July and August. This change was soon
extended to the whole season, and a professional Bowler was
engaged. The matches between the Club Elevens gradually
diminished in frequency, until, sometimes, as on July 31st,
1845, the game consisted of a 'Single Wicket Match, three on a
side, and a Jack on both sides;' frequently the Minutes do not
even mention 'a single Wicket Match.'

In other words, at the very time when the Ladies' Days
were enjoying tremendous popularity and taking up much
of the energy of the club's committee, the enthusiasm for
cricket was such that there was some difficulty getting
enough players to put *any* sort of a match together.
Even when full-scale matches were organized, inevitably
'Ladies' Days were fixed for these meetings', and they
seem to have been compulsory addenda to the games
which Teignbridge played with other clubs.

The cricket, in short, was not too terribly much more
than a good excuse for the socializing and the drinking –
although, with ladies present, the drinking was no doubt
decorous. But even when the cricket has been by far the
more important of the two aspects, the drinking seems to
have been a fairly necessary adjunct at all levels and
through all ages. Who else but a cricketer (it was John
Nyren) would have been capable of waxing so eloquently
on the subject of cricket's essential lubrication?

The ale too! barleycorn such as would put the souls of three
butchers into one weaver. Ale that would flare like turpentine –
genuine Boniface! This immortal viand (for it was more than
liquor) was vended at twopence per pint.

By a strange coincidence, I'm trying to remember this
quote exactly, sitting with a bunch of the others in the

'Two Mile Oak', when Willy starts telling a joke that complements it. '. . . So this drunk says to the barman, "I'll have a pint of lager, pleashe," and the barman just says: "Piss off!" "All right," says the drunk, "I'll have bitter instead." . . .' The jest makes me think of the way that times have changed. Today I suppose you can easily pay a quid for a pint of lager, while in Nyren's time an 'immortal viand' was twopence a pint. For the cost of a pint of lager today Nyren could have had . . . my God! Fifteen gallons! And possibly did.

'It's two o'clock,' Mitch announces suddenly, cutting through the rest of the conversation. 'We'd best get on down to the ground.'

As we go, I notice idly that the conversation is that much more fluid, the movements that much more deliberate, among several members of our happy little bunch. If we bat first, it's likely to be a 'tail-enders' match' – that is, one in which most of the important run-scoring will be done by the lower half of the batting order, because those players will have sobered up enough to play better (rather than worse) than usual. Beer-affected matches can cause the most interesting upsets in the club's seasonal statistics: a number eleven hitting a happy 10 or 15 not out can find himself suddenly launched from the bottom of the averages to somewhere near the top. But the number elevens, at our level of cricket, are not totally unused to experiencing the odd moment of glory. Our friend Bill Pullen – who adds poetry and songsmithery to his skills as a cricketer – sums it up neatly in a verse to be sung to the obvious tune by tail-enders everywhere:

> Show me the way to go home.
> ,I'm tired and I want to go to bed.
> I held a little catch just three hours ago

> And it's gone right to my head:
> Had twenty yards to run –
> I was blinded by the sun –
> But I held on tight
>   and got free drinks all night
> Now show me the way to go home.

In his famous book *The Best Loved Game* (1979) Geoffrey
Moorhouse records a match he watched, during the 1978
Village Championship, between Aston Rowant (population 700), the home side, and Tiddington (population
800), both villages being in Oxfordshire. Aston batted
first, and in their 40 overs made a comfortable 177 for 6,
aided by a more than merely respectable 107 not out
from their opener, McQueen. In their response, it was
soon pretty obvious that Tiddington had very little hope
of overhauling this total – at least until their number ten,
Pykett, whom Moorhouse rather patronizingly describes
as 'the farmer's boy', strode to the wicket, his long hair
held back in place by a blue scarf tied McEnroe-style.

He swipes, with a kind of straight drive, at the first two balls he
receives and gets a couple of runs off the second. Possibly
deciding that a cross-batted clout might improve on this, he
launches the whole of himself at the third ball, spins himself
round through (I'll swear) 360 degrees, and in doing so knocks
himself flat off the meat of the bat.

Does this mean that the heroic batsman will retire injured,
as one of the namby-pamby Test-cricketing crowd might
do? Not a bit of it: at our level of cricket minor injuries
such as broken arms and legs are not deemed sufficient
cause for premature retirement. (I have myself bowled
with a broken rib – but this was because bowling was the
only activity that didn't cause me severe agony.)

Motherly voices are still anxious when the batsman stands again
and indicates his intention to carry on. He gets a great cheer

from everybody at this. And another, when he hits the next ball for 4. There is no stopping him after that, as he mows the Aston bowlers all round the little field. This is not a farmer's boy from Tiddington at all: it is another Lord Peter Wimsey who, it will be recalled, was stung by a fast ball on the elbow joint and then proceeded to punish the bowling for the offence.

This is, of course, the late-order batsman's dream: to succeed brilliantly where the more recognized, higher-order batsmen have so dismally failed. In one match in which I played, the number eleven, despite the diversity of conditions ranged against him – he wore spectacles, it was raining, the last time that he had reached double figures antedated living memory – cheerfully stroked 27 not out in double-quick time, being easily our highest scorer and very nearly saving the match for us.

In another game the tail of our team wagged impressively, and thereby won the contest for us – but that was a rather different affair: a booze-affected match. In accordance with time-honoured cricketing tradition, we had all had an extensive 'net practice' beforehand in Newton Abbot's celebrated Cider Bar (believed to be the only one in the country, for connoisseurs of such things) and were distinctly ebullient by the time we reached the pitch. We batted first, and the score-book was to give a dramatic testimony to the average amount of time it takes a low-grade cricketer to sober up. The first few batsmen got ducks and, if they were lucky, singles; the next few got fives and sixes; and the tail-enders went in there, thought of the *Boys' Own Paper*, and scored rapid twenties and twenty-fives, mostly in boundaries. The defeated opposition must have thought that we'd patronizingly reversed the batting order so as to make more of a match out of it.

Such things can get out of hand, however. Many years ago I played for a company team where free beer and spirits were laid on at every match in astonishing quantities: since the stuff was free, it was accordingly drunk in astonishing quantities, too. Tea, by contrast, was not provided, so experienced camp-followers would arrive with thermos flasks – contrary to popular legend, on a cold day a shot of spirits is more likely to give you hypothermia than a deep inner warmth. The players themselves, who at least had the advantage of running around rather than sitting still pretending to watch with an educated interest, suffered no such constraints. The matches almost always ended in chaos. The curious thing is that they weren't even fun.

Today, however, such scenes of dissolution are unlikely: after all, we're playing a team of doctors, who presumably are going to be alert against the risks of irreversible liver damage . . . or, at least, that's the theory. Actually, as we learn while we're chucking the ball around before the game, the bit about them being doctors is largely theoretical, too. Their captain, on being questioned, admits that not *all* of the team are medicos – which doesn't surprise us, since some of them look as if they're demon cricketers on the Grant's Second Law principle. In fact, the captain continues, possibly less than half of them are involved in the medical profession. To be technical, and not to put too fine a point upon it, if you added up all the medicos in the team you'd get a total not unadjacent to, er, one. Himself. Later on, as we shall find, this total will be reduced still further, because he will depart hastily from the field in response to an urgent summons on his bleeper.

'You do realize,' says Mitch wrathfully, 'that if one of us breaks a leg none of them buggers will know any more than we do what to do about it?' With practised ease he reaches above his head to take a catch, but misses it completely.

'You're soft,' says Rudolph.

Rudolph's right. A couple of hundred years ago people were playing cricket who lacked the full complement of limbs to be broken. It's rather sick, I suppose, but matches contested between, for example, a team of one-legged men and a team of one-armed men were popular spectator events – and not especially uncommon. Just before our blood boils at the idea of freak shows like this, we ought to remember that the effect of such games was not entirely bad: being a cripple in the seventeeth and eighteenth centuries was not a lot of fun, and the money the players could earn must have come in very useful. Still, there is something curiously stomach-wrenching in coming across a record of such a game played in 1811, where rain stopped play because the one-legged players were too seriously hampered: they simply could not cope with the slippery ground, three of them breaking their wooden legs in the shambles.

Other novelty matches were popular, too, including games between teams of women. It says something for the social climate of the times that all-female games were freak-shows just as much as those between cripples. A somewhat rarer variant is described in this advertisement from the *Kentish Gazette* of 29 April 1794:

Cricketing on Horseback
A very singular game of cricket will be played on Tuesday the 6th of May in Linsted Park between the Gentlemen of the Hill and the Gentlemen of the Dale, for one guinea a man. The whole to be performed on horseback. To begin at 9 o'clock, and the game to be played out. A good ordinary on the ground by John Hogben.

Early-morning matches were popular amongst those whose employment obviated their playing the great game during more civilized hours. One of the most famous clubs to be involved in such activities was the Early Bird CC, founded in 1897, made up of butlers and other servants; they played in Battersea Park, starting at 5·30 in the morning. But they were not alone, and nor were they the most masochistic of such clubs, as an 1870 handbill tells us:

Novel Match
A Cricket Match between the Upper Mitcham Early Rising Association versus Lower Mitcham Peep o' Day Club will be played on Lower Mitcham Green on Wednesday mornings July 6th and 13th, 1870. Wickets will be pitched at 3·30 A.M. Play to commence at 4·00 precisely. Stumps to be drawn at 7 o'clock each morning.

Mind you, we mustn't forget that in general people also went to bed much earlier in those days, not having sophisticated late-night television programming to tempt them into sitting up late to read a book instead.

The coin has been tossed, and we're batting first. Mitch and Jonathan are already buckling on their pads, while Willy regales them with stories about batsmen he's known who've had their skulls fractured by lethal Plymouth medical bowlers. The Quakkers are practising throwing the ball in to the wicket-keeper, while we ourselves are still feverishly practising our throwing and catching – not just because we manifestly need every bit of practice we can get but also to try to make sure that Vince's eye doesn't catch any of us to appoint as 'volunteers' for umpiring or scoreboard duty. Naturally enough, he eventually selects these unwilling officials from what Robert Holles, in his entertaining *The Guide to Real Village Cricket* (1983), calls 'the gang of four' – that is, the last four in the batting order who, by contrast with the 'gang of seven', are also called upon to bowl rather less frequently than they ought to be.

So, as I don my white coat and look at the 'gang of seven' continuing to mis-throw and drop catches in the outfield, my mind turns vengefully to J. M. Barrie's list of useful captainly tips to the Allahakbarries – especially to rule number one:

1. Don't practise on an opponent's ground before match begins. This can only give them confidence.
2. Each man, when he goes in, to tap the ground with his bat.
3. Should you hit the ball, run at once. Don't stop to cheer.
4. No batsman is allowed to choose his own bowler. You needn't think it.
5. Partridge, when bowling, keep your eye on square-leg.
6. Square-leg, when Partridge is bowling: Keep your eye on him.
7. If bowled first ball, pretend that you only came out for the fun of the thing, and then go away and sit by yourself behind the hedge.

(J. B. Partridge, who features so ostentatiously in this set of rules, seems to have been an expert in the gentle art of scoring leg-byes: 'His position at the wickets is easy and alert, and he has a large variety of strokes, but he is perhaps best with his right leg. He plays with a very straight pad.')

Vengeful thoughts are all very well, but they don't do terribly much to alleviate the tedium of umpiring: the only thing that can do that is a plethora of no-balls, wickets falling, tight run-out decisions, and so on. Today, since I'm a bit fed up and rather anxious about whether or not I should have had a pee before coming out to the wicket, the bowlers should have something of a field day. Since Rudolph, who can always be relied upon to give a few controversial lbw decisions, is sharing the first duty with me, the early West Country Publishers' CC batsmen should, if only they knew it, curtail any misplaced optimism which they might have. Rudolph and I may not regularly emulate Michael Parkinson's father, and appeal on behalf of the bowler, but . . .

In an essay in *The Twelfth Man* (edited by Martin Boddey, 1971) Garry Marsh recalls a match in which he played for the Stage Cricket Club during 1932, and has a few terse words on the subject of the honesty of hostile umpires. That's right: 'honesty', not dishonesty.

The problem on this occasion was that the opposition had a battery of six or eight devastatingly fast bowlers, and the pitch was, shall we say, perhaps a little less than it should have been. Marsh, as captain, decided to open the batting, on the principle that he would be out almost immediately and then could relax happily in the sun watching the carnage.

The first ball he didn't actually see: he just felt it hurtle past his ear and simultaneously heard it slap into the wicket-keeper's gloves some considerable distance behind. The second struck him agonizingly in the chest, and the over-eager bowler reflexively appealed. Marsh did the decent thing and walked – only to be recalled when he was halfway to the pavilion by a stern umpire, who refused point-blank to give him out.

To retire without losing one's wicket would be the path of cowardice, of course – but Marsh found that getting out wasn't quite as easy as he'd thought it would be. The bowlers, perhaps intent on giving Douglas Jardine a few ideas for the upcoming winter tour of Australia, seemed to have few ambitions connected with hitting the stumps. They were instead in quest of fractures, bruises, gore and blood. Marsh's partner at the other end actually succeeded in scoring four leg-byes off his head. And, despite his every effort, Marsh's wicket remained stubbornly intact.

Finally he was hit on the foot by a particularly vicious over-pitched ball. Cursing with agony, he collapsed to the ground – but an isolated, lucid part of his mind still had just enough control left to enable him to swing his bat round to shatter the stumps. As he lay there writhing piteously, the umpire at last relented and held up his finger.

What we don't know is whether or not the umpire ever realized that the player who had shouted 'How's that!' was the batsman himself.

In his celebrated book *A Pattern of Islands* (1952), about his experiences as a Briton residing in the Gilbert and Ellice Islands, Arthur Grimble has a fair amount to say on the subject of local cricket – concentrating much of his attention on the difficulties of umpiring. These difficulties were not exclusively born out of such matters as interpretation of the Laws: sometimes the umpires didn't so much have problems thrust upon 'em as did their best to achieve them. In one match the incumbent batsman and the umpire were rivals for the affections of one of the local girls. The umpire tried first of all to give the batsman out on the grounds that he had BO; this failing, he next tried to dismiss him lbw to a ball that was palpably missing the leg stump (the umpire had to be overruled by the fielding side); and finally, when the naturally ruffled player was clean bowled, his rival in love followed him all the way to the pavilion screeching 'Ouchi!' (Out!), jumping up and down with glee, and employing a diversity of unflattering adjectives.

In another game reported by Grimble there was a run-out confusion: when the two batsmen collided in the middle of the pitch and collapsed to the ground, the difference in their running abilities had been such that one was halfway through taking the fifth run while the other was still on the third. In the end it was decreed that the slower of the two sportsmen had been the one to be run out – especially since he had been badly winded in the crash, and so would anyway have had difficulty in continuing.

And then, says Grimble, there was the perennial enigma of 'when is a catch not a catch?':

One Abakuka so played a rising ball that it span up his arm and, by some fluke, lodged inside the yellow and purple shirt with which he was honouring our game. Swiftly the wicket keeper darted forward and grappled with him, intending to seize the ball and so catch him out. After a severe struggle, Abakuka escaped and fled. The whole field gave chase. The fugitive, hampered by pads donned upside down (to protect his insteps from full-pitchers), was overtaken on the boundary. Even handicapped as he was, he would hardly have been caught had he not tried there, by standing on his head, to decant the ball from his shirt-front; and though held, feet in air, he resisted the interference with such fury that it took all that eleven masses of brown brawn could do to persuade the leather from his bosom. After so gallant a fight, it would have been sad to judge him out. Fortunately, we were saved the pain, as he was carried from the field on a stretcher.

Grimble's tale is vaguely reminiscent of an event which took place in England, at a rather higher level of the game, in 1946. The Surrey player Alf Gover, fielding at slip in a match against the Combined Services, was putting on his jersey (and thus effectively blind) when the ball was accurately snicked in such a way that it lodged neatly between his thighs. The appeal was made and the catch was given. The bowler was jubilant – because it was the first wicket he had ever taken in first-class cricket. The bowler's name? Jim Laker.

Umpires can be either hostile or friendly, and the reasons for their partisan behaviour need not always be connected with conscious dishonesty. In his *A Yorkshire Boyhood* (1983) Roy Hattersley comes up with a recollection that epitomizes the problem:

Indeed had my father not offered to become our regular umpire (to 'keep an eye on things', as I heard my mother say in the hall as she instructed him to volunteer) the Wadsley Church Youth Club CC might have launched my longed-for professional cricket career. My father was desperate for me to succeed as a boy cricketer. But he also regarded it as his duty to compensate for his natural bias in my favour by giving me out in response to every appeal. His attitude did more for his reputation as a man of honour than it did for me as a batsman. In the end my place in the side was only saved by an injury he sustained as the result of a wild attempt at a run-out hitting him on the foot. His ankle was too swollen to support him through two innings, so his place was taken by a Mr Stringfellow, the virtually blind father of our wicket-keeper. Mr Stringfellow was less inhibited in his attitude towards his son. And the only way in which he could be sure of never dismissing the object of his paternal loyalty was to cry 'not out' in response to any appeal against all the shadowy figures at the far end of the wicket.

Tales of partisan umpires are of course legion – we've already encountered a few – but fathers seem to be particularly notorious in this respect. Michael Parkinson has written on several occasions of his father's umpiring skills when young Michael was at the wicket, and in *Cricket Mad* (1969) he recounts a way in which his father was able to influence the outcome even when not standing in the white coat. Both of them were batting in a match which their team seemed certain to lose. The boy Michael prepared nervously to face a demonic fast bowler on a wicket that 'had seen better days' – or even, perhaps, hadn't. At the nonstriker's end Parkinson Senior retreated with the bowler all the way back to his mark and then, despite the paceman's protests, ran in alongside him, pads flapping. As the umpire agreed when consulted, there's nothing actually in the Laws to say that you *can't* do this.

Three wides later the bowler complained again, this time in the most highly decorative language. Parkinson

Senior promptly appealed to the umpire, asserting that these were not the sort of words which should be used in front of a mere child such as son Michael. The umpire considered the matter and then agreed – awarding the match to the Parkinsons' team.

One detects just a whiff of bias on the umpire's part – and it's rather alarming to find that such 'sportsmanship' extends even into the hallowed grounds of clerical matches. John Trevisick, who has organized the *Church Times* competition since its inception, has written to me that

Cricketing parsons are no different from other human beings – at least on the cricket field – and not least in the art of gamesmanship.

One of the rules of the competition states that an eligible player must possess the Bishop's licence to officiate in his diocese – he could be other than a vicar or a rector; e.g., a school or prison chaplain, or a teacher. There have been attempts to side-track this rule, but they have not succeeded.

Professional umpires are employed for the competition's final, but some strange things have happened in regional matches – for example, an ordained umpire fiddling the time at which an innings should close, and thereby making sure that his own side won. There was one match which the umpire insisted should continue – on a well known county ground – in semidarkness and with the street-lights aglow. Parsons are not above giving very doubtful decisions at the wicket in favour of their friends. Human nature covers a wide canvas!

Indeed it does: the gentlemen of the cloth are as capable of 'overenthusiasm' as the rest of us. In an 1856 match between Ilkeston and Hathern, stumps were to be drawn by 6·00 P.M. The task of scoring 113 runs to win the match by that time seemed beyond the Ilkeston team, although they were making a brave effort at it. As the hands of the nearby church clock came closer and closer to the fateful 6·00 position, it struck some of the Ilkeston supporters that if only . . .

With the vicar's permission, two small lads were despatched to the church, one to keep watch and one to hold the pendulum for a few extra seconds at the end of each swing. Unfortunately the ruse was in due course discovered: the bowling team could hardly help but notice that, despite their own delaying tactics, they seemed to be getting through their overs really rather more quickly than sense would allow. In the end the umpires were forced to uproot the stumps and declare the result a draw.

In fact, I very soon discover that the Quakkers do not in any way require the willing assistance of either myself or Rudolph. Their bowlers are getting our major batsmen totally snarled up by using such dubious measures as bowling accurately towards the stumps. Our players, not used to this sort of thing, are forming a steady parade of hopefuls striding to the wicket and then, very shortly afterwards, slouching disconsolately away again. The net result is that I have to stand out there in the cold for a very much shorter period than I had initially thought I was going to. Soon Rudolph and I are happily padding up. The burning question is: will there be time for a quick fag before the next two wickets have fallen?

But – but what's this? Ronnie, whose scores for the club to date have had only the single virtue of consistency, seems to be surviving rather a long time at the crease. In fact – yes, that snick he's just hit means that for the first time in the season he's got an average. Someone tries, out loud, to calculate what 1 divided by 9 is in decimals, but the mathematician is too slow, because Ronnie has just opened his shoulders and hit a two. Much more of this and he'll become insufferable. My God! That was a genuine boundary! What the devil's got into the man?

Of course, this dramatic partnership can't last much longer. The batsman at the other end, one of the few of us to display a full range of classy strokes and to regularly accumulate runs, is clean bowled, leaving Ronnie out there, bat on his shoulder, smugly surveying the world around him, emperor for a day. Tapping my bat on the ground, just like J. M. Barrie told me to, I wander out to join him, pausing occasionally to give the bat a Botham-esque, windmill-like 360-degree swing at arm's length.

'I think we ought to have a quick chat about tactics,' I say to Ronnie. 'Not because I can think of any, but just to impress the opposition.'

'Yeah,' says Ronnie with the easy grin of a centurion. 'The only trouble is that I can't think of effing any either.'

'Tell you what,' I say, 'shall we just try to hit the bloody thing as far as possible?'

'That sounds OK to me.'

Nodding sagely to each other, and muttering 'tactic 47B' just loudly enough for the nearby fielders to hear, we separate. I make a point of digging as deep and elaborate a crease for myself as possible, survey the fielders carefully to make sure the opposition think I have a remote idea of where the ball might go in the event of my making contact with it, ask silly mid-on if he really wants to stay there (generally speaking, even if I miss the first ball I face, any silly mid-on moves back about twenty-five yards, such is the . . . er . . . strength of my on-side play), exchange a jest with the wicket-keeper (I have no direct evidence of this, but I'm sure it disrupts any 'keeper's concentration), and settle down to face my first ball. This is to be delivered by their fiery opening bowler, who has been brought back for a second spell. This circumstance is not quite as frightening as you might think, because he's damaged his leg and is now reduced to sending down slowish off-spinners that don't actually turn. Confidence flows through me.

Here comes the ball. It's slow, it's easy, my bat lifts and -- the bloody ball turns. An impertinent snicking noise sounds behind me as the ball rolls casually against the stumps, dislodging a single bail. As I drift back to the pavilion I think of the times I've felt the wind sing on the willow blade and seen the ball go careering away to the boundary (curiously enough, always the leg-side one), and reflect bitterly that that delicious sensation is not going to be mine today – or, indeed, until next spring, because the barbecue match is the last of the 1984 season.

There is perhaps no joy to equal that of hitting the ball a very great distance, especially if you're a bowler. It doesn't matter if you've played with a straight bat or not, if you've produced a glorious on drive or simply clouted the damn' thing with your eyes shut, when you see the ball vanishing over the back of the pavilion or into the next field. There is probably, by contrast, no misery greater than being out first ball when you had imagined yourself launching such a magnificent stroke. Still, my lot could be worse. The actor Trevor Howard had a much more frustrating golden duck than most of the rest of us have ever experienced. In order to play in a match in Buxton, he had got up at 5·00 in the morning and travelled about 180 miles. Fate rewarded his dedication harshly.

But big hitting, that's another matter.

In 1980, in the Lancashire League, Bacup were playing Ramsbottom and, for Bacup at least, it was an important match: they were having a good season, and a victory would put them within striking distance of the top of the table. They batted well, and it soon became clear that

Ramsbottom were going to be unable to pass the Bacup score within the allotted 40 overs.

In the Lancashire League, the winning team can gain an extra point if it succeeds in skittling out the opposition in the process, and so the Bacup skipper, Roger Law, decided that it would be a good plan to try to 'buy' a few wickets by putting on the slowest of slow spinners. The wheeze seemed to be working, until one of the tail-end sloggers remembered that the best way of dealing with slow spinners is to hit the ball clear over the boundary rope, so that no one can catch it. Putting the theory at least temporarily into practice, he succeeded in shattering the windscreen of one of the cars parked near the boundary. In due course, however, despite such temporary setbacks, Bacup won the match comfortably enough.

Afterwards Law was walking back to the changing rooms when he passed the car that had suffered the damage. Inside was a red-faced and furious owner, clearing up all the pieces of smashed glass and trying to deal with his sagging, snowy windscreen.

'All right?' said Law with shy courtesy.

'All bloody *right*?' shouted the car owner, sticking his head through the gap in his windscreen. 'Didn't you hear me? Three times I told you to take that bugger off!'

Cars are favourite targets of the sloggers: it's always puzzled me why people seem so relaxed about parking their cars within a mere forty or fifty yards of the crease. It's not just a question of a brutish six breaking the windows: a mis-hit four can have the ball bouncing and tumbling along to cause healthy damage to the bodywork. Even in the professional grounds, however, where the vehicles are carefully tucked away in carparks at a considerable distance from the pitch, safety is not assured. (Don't park your car at the Taunton ground, for example!) Once upon a time the Hon. Charles Lyttelton (later to become Lord Cobham) was playing in a club match in Canterbury when he hit an enormous six right over the stand. The ball dropped out of sight into the car park, and a few moments later there was the cheery sound of smashing glass. Lyttelton laughed merrily: it's always fun to do a lot of damage with a doughty hit. His laughter faded later, when someone explained to him that the car in question had been his own . . .

The garnering of runs from big hits can be helped by factors other than the sheer might of the shot. In his contribution to a collection of reminiscences concerning the Devon Dumplings CC, Wilfrid Harrison of the Dorset Rangers recollects a few of the features of the matches the two clubs had played against each other, one of which is pertinent here; he concludes with a rallying cry that is as relevant to all low-level cricketers today as it was in 1952, when it was penned:

Certain episodes come back to me, as, for instance, in 1910 when, in addition to taking no wickets and making a 'pair', I had my little finger badly broken. Incidentally that finger has been no use ever since! On another occasion I remember two sixes being scored (all run) off consecutive balls. I was the unfortunate fielder who had to pursue the ball to within a few yards of the square-leg boundary. In 1938 one of our side hired a wireless and while we sat in the pavilion with sea-gulls wading knee-deep on the wicket and rain pouring down, we listened to Hutton's record Test score at the Oval and the commentator's remarks about the hot sun and the brilliant weather! . . .

There is no doubt that [friendly] cricket is the most enjoyable of all. It is completely carefree: no first innings points, no championship table to worry about, no petty parochial rivalry, and each side going all out for a definite finish. Long may it continue to flourish!

Alas, like myself, Rudolph has failed to score two sixes, all run or otherwise, off consecutive balls, and our innings has come to an end. 'I don't know why I bother,' storms Rudolph as he comes off, throwing his bat in the general direction of the kit-bag. 'I don't even *like* this bloody game any more,' he adds as usual, and then he continues in his familiar vein: 'This is the last time I'm playing, I tell you. I'm just giving it up next season. I've had enough. That's it. Where the hell's my pipe?'

He'll be back next season, I have no fear – and earnestly hope. But his temporary hatred for the finest game is an echo of some of the more permanent loathings for it that have been voiced down the long years. Some of these were born from the conviction that cricket, being fun, should not be played on a Sunday – or, to be more charitable and assume that the game's pious critics were being less bigoted, perhaps what really concerned them was the atmosphere of heavy betting which surrounded many matches in the sport's early days: at least the devout did not criticize cricket *per se*. Not so the author of a piece which appeared in the *Gentlemen's Magazine* in September 1743. It's worth looking at this in some length, if only to be staggered by its sheer vitriol. Is this – can this be – the same game that we all love so much?

In diversions as well as business, circumstances alter things mightily, and what in one man may be decent, may in another be ridiculous; what is innocent in one light may be quite the contrary in another; nor is it at all impossible that exercise may be strained too far. A journeyman shoemaker may play from five o'clock on Saturday in the afternoon till it is dark at skittles, provided he has worked all the rest of the week. Yet I can't say it would but shock me a little if I saw honest Crispin tipping against a member of each House of Parliament. All diversions at exercises have certain bounds as to expense, and when they exceed this it is an evil in itself and justly liable to censure. Upon that reason are not all the laws against family founded. Are not these the chief – that they break in upon your business, expose people to great dangers, and cherish a spirit of covetousness, in a way directly opposed to industry? The most wholesome exercise and the most innocent diversion may change its nature entirely if people, for the sake of gratifying their humour keep unfit company. I have been led into these reflections, which are certainly just in themselves, by some odd stories I have heard of cricket matches, which I own, however, to be so strange and incredible that, if I had not received them from eye-witnesses, I could never have yielded to them any belief. Is it not a very wild thing to be as serious in making such a match as in the most material occurrences in life? Would it not be extremely odd to see lords and gentlemen, clergymen and lawyers, associating themselves with butchers and cobblers in pursuit of their diversions? or can there be anything more absurd than making such matches for the sake of profit, which is to be shared amongst people, so remote in their quality and circumstances? Cricket is certainly a very innocent and wholesome exercise, yet it may be absurd if either great or little people make it their business. It is grossly absurd when it is made the subject of public advertisement to draw together great crowds of people who ought, all of them, to be somewhere else. Noblemen, gentlemen and clergymen have certainly the right to divert themselves in what manner they think fit, nor do I dispute their privilege of making butchers, cobblers, or tinkers their companions, provided they are gratified to keep them company. But I very much doubt whether they have any right to invite thousands of people to be spectators of their agility, at the expense of their duty and honesty. The time of people of fashion may be, indeed, of little value, but in a trading country, the time of the meanest man ought to be of some worth to himself and to the community. The diversion of cricket may be proper in holiday time and in the country; but upon days when men ought to be busy, and in the neighbourhood of a great city, it is not only improper but mischievous to a high degree. It draws numbers of people away from their employment to the ruin of their families. It brings together crowds of apprentices and servants whose time is not their own. It propagates a spirit of idleness at a juncture when, with the utmost industry, our debts, taxes, and decay of trade will scarce allow us to get bread. It is a most notorious breach of the laws, as it gives the most open encouragement to gaming – the advertisements most impudently reciting that great sums are laid, so that some people are so little ashamed of breaking the laws they had a hand in making that they give public notice of it.

The spleenful author seems to be attacking cricket because of the attendant gambling (a reasonable viewpoint), because of the behaviour, actual or possible, of the spectators (which is rather like blaming the game of football for the hooligans who go along to matches to smash each other's skulls in), and because of the way in which it encourages people from all walks of life to meet and interact as equals – something which I've always thought was one of cricket's great virtues. But the correspondent in the *Gentlemen's Magazine* was rather out on a limb – although John Ford, who gives this extract in his *Cricket: A Social History 1700–1835* (1972), mentions also such events as the dispersal of a cricket match in 1726 by a JP who thought that the whole affair was simply an excuse for congregating a revolutionary mob. When the subject was not just cricket but *women* playing cricket, however, far more of the 'gentlemen' were prepared to dip their pens in vitriol and make a few contributions to the debate. In 1833 we find, for example, the *Nottingham Review* writing in terms that are positively shocked:

Last week, at Sileby feast, the women so far forgot themselves as to enter upon a game of cricket, and by their deportment as well as frequent applications to the tankard, they rendered themselves objects such as no husband, brother, parent, or lover could contemplate with any degree of satisfaction.

Cricketing males, of course, never allowed themselves 'frequent applications to the tankard' and, even if they did, would still have been objects of veneration to their wives, sisters, parents and lovers, I suppose. However, in amongst all of this sort of hostility there were some more friendly comments. Here is *Monthly Magazine or British*

Register writing in October 1811 of a match which had been arranged at Ball's Pond, Middlesex:

A grand cricket match has been played this month between eleven women of Surrey and eleven women of Hampshire for 500 guineas. The combatants were dressed in loose trowsers with short fringed petticoats descending to the knees, and light flannel waistcoats with sashes round the waist. The performers were all ages and sizes, from fourteen years to upwards of fifty, and were distinguished by club ribbons: royal purple for Hampshire; orange and blue for Surrey.

Well, now at least we know how the ladies were dressed. To find out about the cricket we have to turn instead to the *Sporting Magazine* (which, incidentally, disagrees with the *Monthly Magazine or British Register* about the colours the teams wore):

Very excellent play took place on Wednesday, one of the Hampshire lasses made forty-one innings before she was thrown out; and at the conclusion of the day's sport, the Hampshire eleven were 81 ahead – the unfavourableness of the weather prevented any more sport that day, though the ground was filled with spectators. On the following day, the Surrey lasses kept the field with great success; and on Monday the 7th, being the last day to decide the contest, an unusual assemblage of elegant persons were on the ground. At three o'clock the match was won by the Hampshire lasses, who not being willing to leave the field at so early an hour, and having only won by two innings [runs], they played a single, in which they were also successful. Afterwards they marched in triumph to the Angel at Islington, where a handsome entertainment had been provided for them, by the Noblemen that made the match.

Both of these two newspapers display at least a trace of being patronizing; however, at least their accounts aren't out-and-out hostile. Unfortunately, male-piggery on the subject of female cricket is still pretty rampant at all levels of the game – not least, alas, at the more lowly levels. The male-chauvinist-pig elements in cricket simply take it as axiomatic that women are incapable of understanding, let alone playing, the noble sport. How else would the probably apocryphal tale circulate of the batsman who returned home to his girlfriend after a less than satisfactory day's play?

'Did you have a good day?' she said, keen to show becoming interest in her true love's *raison d'être*.

'Bloody awful,' he replied. 'I was run out for a duck.' He sank gloomily into the armchair and stared at the flowers on the wallpaper.

Putting her arm around his shoulder, she said comfortingly: 'Well, I expect it was a very good ball.'

Thigh-slapping stuff, huh?

What the boneheads fail to remember is that women have made some fundamental contributions to the game. Round-arm bowling, for example, was certainly introduced to cricket thanks to a woman, although there is some controversy as to who that woman actually was. The two main candidates are Mrs Lambert and Christina Willes. One or the other – we shall call them jointly 'Wilbert' – used to help William Lambert (the husband) or John Willes (the brother) to practise their strokes by bowling to them in the barn. At this time, around the beginning of the nineteenth century, women generally wore full skirts, and so Wilbert found great difficulty in bowling in the underarm style of the day. And so, naturally enough, she was forced to adopt the round-arm method of delivery; the batsman, whichever of the two men he was (and he might even have been both, independently), was quick to recognize the potential of this new way of bowling. The rest is history.

John Willes, Christina's brother, fought for a decade and a half to have round-arm bowling recognized as legitimate. Indeed, he must have been a man of extraordinary persistence, because throughout all that long period he had to put up with being regularly no-balled because of his unorthodox bowling action. It's surprising, too, that captains picked him in light of the prospect of so many no-balls being awarded. It must have been a case of sheer merit on his part – and, indeed, the local saying of the time was that 'Willes, his sister and his dog [which fielded] could beat any eleven in England'.

Women's cricket goes back a pretty long way. A manuscript, dated 1344, in the Bodleian Library has a picture of a nun holding a ball and apparently preparing to bowl it at a monk who is armed with something that looks suspiciously like a cricket bat; four 'fielders' – two monks and two nuns – are seemingly waiting for the catch. Of course, to say that this is proof of fourteenth-century cricket would be to go too far – they might well be playing some ancestor of rounders, or doing something else altogether. Certainly, though, the women's game seems to be not overwhelmingly younger than the male equivalent. The first recorded century to be scored by a woman came on 11 July 1788, when a Miss S. Norcross made 107 in a match between eleven Maids of Surrey and eleven Married Ladies of Surrey; this was quite a long time after the first recorded women's match, played on 26 July 1745, at Gosden Common in Surrey, although doubtless there were both earlier matches and earlier centuries. In 1931 a woman, Rubina Humphries, in a match between Dalton Ladies and Woodfield Sporting Club, not only took all ten Woodfield wickets for no runs but also scored all the Dalton Ladies' runs. In 1934, at Brisbane, the first women's Test match was played between England and Australia, England winning comfortably by nine wickets. In 1958 the first cricketer of either sex to do the 'double' of 100 runs and 10 wickets in their inaugural Test match was not Ian Botham or Kapil Dev or Imran Khan but the Australian Betty Wilson, against England; two years were to go by before any male cricketer could emulate this feat – this was Alan Davidson, like Wilson an Australian, in 1960 against the West Indies. In 1963 came the first six to be hit in a women's Test match, when England's Rachael Heyhoe Flint did it at the Oval against the Australians. In light of all this prowess, it seems strange that it was not until 1970 that *Wisden* saw fit to make a female cricketer the subject of a special feature: the woman who was so honoured was Enid Bakewell.

The true dyed-in-the-wool male chauvinist pig is of course unimpressed by these statistics: anyone can hit a six against a grot women's bowling attack, he proclaims. But look at the highest women's Test score: 189, by Betty Snowball in 1935, playing for England against New Zealand. Or the highest recorded individual score, 224 not out, made by Mabel Bryant playing for the Visitors against the Residents at Eastbourne in 1901. Or the highest Test innings score, when in 1935 England, playing against New Zealand, made 503 for 5 declared. These are all hefty scores. *Anyone* who can make 224 not out, even when playing against a team of toddlers, is far from being a cricketing slouch – and must also have a fair degree of athletic stamina to back up his or her cricketing skills.

Some female cricketers have been or have become prominent figures. Rachael Heyhoe Flint, mentioned earlier, is nowadays something of a British institution. Lucy Ridsdale, who married prime minister Stanley Baldwin, was a highly enthusiastic cricketer of no mean ability. She said, in fact, that marriage had done much for her performance on the field by reducing her feelings of nervousness: '. . . it was the year that I was married [1892] that I made my best batting average, 62 runs for the season.' Any batsman, male or female, amateur or professional, would be quite pleased to end the season with an average of 62. And yet women are still barred from many areas of our most hallowed grounds!

And women have, too, excelled in writing about cricket. While A. G. Macdonell's cricket match from *England, Their England* (1933) is undoubtedly the best known and most reprinted account of all, a strong second is the description provided by Mary Russell Mitford in *Our Village* a century earlier, in 1832. Her full account is available in countless editions, so I don't plan to repeat all of it here – just enough to give a flavour, and to show that things haven't changed all that much in lowly cricket over the last one hundred and fifty years or so.

The village has been challenged to a game of cricket by the neighbouring hamlet of B., and thoroughly expects to be comprehensively massacred. Still, pride is pride . . . but matters are made worse by that most frequent of low-level cricket disasters: the best player, Jem Brown, fails to turn up – seduced away from his loyalties by the temptations of a fair woman, who has written to him:

Mistur browne this is to Inform you that oure parish plays bramley men next monty is a week, i think we shall lose without yew, from your humbell servant to command

Mary Allen.

Some of the villagers are touched by the romance of it all – Jem has walked twelve miles at the summons of his true love – but the true cricketers are less than amused. It is with gloomy hearts and dire premonitions that they gird themselves to face the battle with the stalwarts of B.

But, alas! I have been so long settling my preliminaries, that I have left myself no room for the detail of our victory, and must squeeze the account of our grand achievements into as little compass as Cowley, when he crammed the names of eleven of his mistresses into the narrow space of four eight-syllable lines. *They* began the warfare – those boastful men of B. And what think you, gentle reader, was the amount of their innings? These challengers – the famous eleven – how many did they get? Think! imagine! guess! – You cannot? – Well! – they got twenty-two, or rather, they got twenty; for two of theirs were short notches, and would never have been allowed, only that, seeing what they were made of, we and our umpires were not particular – They should have had twenty more if they had chosen to claim them. Oh, how well we fielded! and how well we bowled! our good play had quite as much to do with their miserable failure as their bad. Samuel Long is a slow bowler, George Simmons a fast one, and the change from Long's lobbing to Simmons' fast balls posed them completely. Poor simpletons! they were always wrong, expecting the slow for the quick, and the quick for the slow. Well, we went in. And what were our innings? Guess again! – guess! A hundred and sixty-nine! in spite of soaking showers, and wretched ground, where the ball would not run a yard, we headed them by a hundred and forty-seven; and then they gave in, as well they might. William Grey pressed them to try another innings. 'There was so much chance,' as he courteously observed, 'in cricket, that advantageous as our position seemed, we might, very possibly, be overtaken. The B. men had better try.' But they were beaten sulky and would not move – to my great disappointment; I wanted to prolong the pleasure of success. What a glorious sensation it is to be for five hours together – winning – winning! always feeling what a whist-player feels when he takes up four honours, seven trumps! Who would think that a little bit of leather and two pieces of wood, had such a delightful and delighting power!

The only drawback on my enjoyment was the failure of the pretty boy, David Willis, who, injudiciously put in first, and playing for the first time in a match amongst men and strangers, who talked to him, and stared at him, was seized with such a fit of shamefaced shyness, that he could scarcely hold his bat, and was bowled out without a stroke, from actual nervousness. 'He will come off that,' Tom Coper says – I am afraid he will. I wonder whether Tom had ever any modesty to lose. Our other modest lad, John Strong, did very well; his length told in fielding and he got good fame. He ran out his mate, Samuel

Long; who, I do believe, but for the excess of Joel's eagerness, would have stayed in till this time, by which exploit he got into sad disgrace; and then he himself got thirty-seven runs, which redeemed his reputation. William Grey made a hit which actually lost the cricket-ball. We think she lodged in a hedge, a quarter of a mile off, but nobody could find her. And George Simmons had nearly lost his shoe, which he tossed away in a passion, for having been caught out, owing to the ball glancing against it. These, together with a very complete somerset of Ben Appleton, our long-stop, who floundered about in the mud, making faces and attitudes as laughable as Grimaldi, none could tell whether by accident or design, were the chief incidents of the scene of action. Amongst the spectators nothing remarkable occurred, beyond the general calamity of two or three drenchings, except that a form, placed by the side of a hedge, under a very insufficient shelter, was knocked into the ditch in a sudden rush of the cricketers to escape a pelting shower, by which means all parties shared the fate of Ben Appleton, some on land and some by water; and that, amidst the scramble, a saucy gipsy of a girl contrived to steal from the knee of the demure and well-apparelled Samuel Long, a smart handkerchief which his careful dame had tied round it to preserve his new (what is the mincing feminine word?) – his new – inexpressibles, thus reversing the story of Desdemona, and causing the new Othello to call aloud for his handkerchief, to the great diversion of the company. And so we parted; the players retired to their supper, and we to our homes; all wet through, all good-humoured and happy – except the losers.

But I think it's the last paragraph of Mitford's account that really sums up for me all that's best about the honest glow of victory which cricket can give its devotees.

Today we are happy too. Hats, with ribands in them, go glancing up and down; and William Grey says, with a proud humility, 'We do not challenge any parish; but if we be challenged we are ready.'

Of course, in Mitford's village cricket match, the women were only there in the subservient roles to which many

men would like, even today, to confine them: as adulating
spectators, as servers of refreshments – as camp-followers.
Curiously, there are plenty of wives and girlfriends who
seem only too happy to go along with this, carrying
out thankless tasks like tending the tea-urn and baking
strangely revolting cakes. In his eloquent *Beyond a
Boundary* (1963) C. L. R. James, possibly the most
interesting of all writers on cricket, tells of a woman's
devotion to her cricketing offspring that goes way beyond
all the normal limits. His Aunt Judith had a son who,
although no great sportsman himself, would every year
organize a festive match at Tunapuna, where the family
lived, and to this game he would invite his friends from
far and wide. After the cricket, the ritual was that they
would all go back to the house, where Aunt Judith would
have been working since the crack of dawn to prepare for
them a magically magnificent feast. But one year things
were a little different:

The friends came, the match was played and then all trooped in
to eat, hungry, noisy and happy. Judith was serving when
suddenly she sat down, saying, 'I am not feeling so well.' She
leaned her head on the table. When they bent over her to find
out what was wrong she was dead. I would guess that she had
been 'not feeling so well' for days, but she was not one to let
that turn her aside from doing what she had to do.

Looking around the pavilion as we sit down hungrily to
our tea, I see several women who, in a small way, are
like James' Aunt Judith. Even my wife, who has a fairly
deep loathing for cricket and a genuinely deep one for
being forced to socialize at matches when she would
much rather be reading a book, several times a season
stuffs into my arms as I leave the house some delicacy
which she has cooked up at colossal expense of time and
money. Last week it was the sausage rolls that were so

spicy and powerful that merely thinking about them can bring the taste back to the tongue – I'm certain there was a fight over the last one – and this week it's a Dundee cake of imposing professionalism. But some of the other camp-followers do so much towards the production of these teas that one almost feels guilty eating them. It's the same in virtually every other cricket club I've come across; and yet all the work seems just to be taken for granted by the doughty fellows themselves. And then, on the occasions that the men burst into print with their reminiscences, it's always just a question of 'thanks to all those lovely ladies – where would we be without their grrrreat teas?', as if women were somehow nothing but cake-baking machines, one step down from being sex-objects; as if the only interaction between women and cricket is to be found in the steam rising out of the aluminium tea-urn.

Pah!

Fed and watered, leaving the dirty plates just like all the other male-chauvinist cricketers do, we trek out onto the cricket field once more. Pat has put on his 'keeper's pads, and it's time to throw the ball as hard as possible directly at his head so that he can practise catching it. Of course, the likelihood of a ball coming straight at him during the game itself is a pretty slender one, but this we ignore.

My mind's hardly on all this, because I'm still feeling a bit guilty about leaving the women to do all the washing up; apart from my own higher feelings, what will Catherine say if she finds out? No, there's more to it than that. When I was a kid, the girls joined in with the boys at cricket, and no one really thought about it; likewise nobody seems to think it strange that I try to keep my daughter supplied with stumps and a bat (and the little swine bowled me out once, too). One of my sisters-in-law played cricket at school – alongside a girl who is now a well known female broadcaster. Yet somehow, when everyone's grown up to adulthood, almost all of the men and, to be honest, most of the women, too, seem to get the idea that cricket's a sport only for the hairier sex. Why?

The children's writer Alison Uttley – author of all those Little Grey Rabbit books and goodness knows how many others besides – was another aspiring child cricketer. To her, 'Cricket and church were alike holy' – and not just because the vicar, a cricket enthusiast if ever there was one, played for the village team ('He couldn't preach, but we forgave him because he played cricket') and introduced the game into such matters as confirmation preparation.

Cricket had been the centre of our lives ever since I can remember. When my brother was about seven and I was nine my father brought us from the market town a set of yellow stumps and bails and a real bat. We had begged and cajoled and wheedled him to get them. Before that we played with a bat my father made, the stable door as a wicket, and the stumps chalked upon it. This involved much argument as to whether the wicket had been hit, much peering at the chalk to see if any was rubbed away. It was a great day when the six brightly painted wickets came out of the market basket, and we held the little bails in our hands and stroked the bat. The smell of the twine on the handle went to our heads like wine. We were nearly delirious with joy as we rubbed the bat with linseed oil from the barn.

My father measured out a small pitch on the little enclosed lawn near the house. We made a hole for the bat, which we euphemistically called the crease, and we began to play a game that never ended. In imagination I still bat there and play tip-and-run, and call to the echoes.

Behind the batting end was the garden wall, the strong old wall with its massive rough stones. It acted as long-stop and saved a fielder. On the off side was our beloved, familiar, friendly wall, where we played see-saw, with a plank over it; where we ran as trains puffing up and down; where we leapt and flew our kites, played shop and five-stones. It, too, was a fielder, but beyond it was the house with its many windows, and we had to make a rule that no ball went over it. Once I brought the doctor's sons home with me from school to play cricket. When three windows had been broken, my father stopped the game and I was shamed before them. The 'on' side had the orchard, which was 'six and out'. It took a long time to climb down the steep face of the wall and to search for the ball in the thick grass under the apple trees, with the pony trotting there, alarmed at the missile, or the cade lamb butting its hard little head at one's legs. There was a time when a hit in the orchard disturbed the bees in the hives and sent them buzzing round our heads. It was not a popular place, and the cricketer immediately put his bat down and helped to find the ball.

The most curious thing about that extract from Uttley's *Cats and Candlesticks* (1948) is that, if you put it in front of the most piggish of male-chauvinist cricketers, he would be totally unable to tell, from the internal evidence, that here was a woman writing about her girlhood, rather than a man writing about his boyhood. Try the test on someone yourself.

Of course some girls – as well as plenty of boys – just plain don't like cricket; a bizarre little mental aberration, but we must be tolerant. Caroline Hill, writing in Allen Synge's first-rate anthology *Strangers' Gallery* (1974), tells of the acme of her school cricketing career: the match which her school played against the much larger nearby establishment, St Mary's. The best that could be hoped for was a draw, but by far the more likely result was an out-and-out thrashing.

Their worst fears seemed likely to be confirmed in the opening over of the match: their 'star' batswoman was out for a duck. All seemed lost until, in the second over, one of the St Mary's bowlers sent down a delivery so lethal that it missed the bat, missed the wicket, and knocked out the two front teeth of the wicket-keeper. By general consensus it was agreed that to continue the match after such a painful mishap would be little short of tasteless, and so the result went down in the scorebooks as a draw – a tooth-affected match, I suppose. Caroline Hill and the rest of the visiting team had, of course, to conceal their elation behind prim little schoolgirl masks of propriety until they got back to school and then – wahey!!

Hill's match has much in common with Mitford's, come to think of it. In both cases the apparently weaker teams come out of the encounter with their pride and honour intact. It doesn't seem to make much difference that in one case the players were male, in the other female.

Yet still the myth persists that women can't, or shouldn't, play cricket. Perhaps the worst chauvinist cricketer of the lot of them was J. M. Barrie – yes, the very same who wrote so lightly and self-mockingly about his own exploits on the cricket pitch. In *The Greenwood Hat* (1930) he included a famous essay which he had written on the subject of ladies at cricket. It must be one of the most patronizing products of any man's pen – and to anyone who suggests that Barrie didn't *mean* to be patronizing, all that one can say is that that makes it even worse. As with Mitford's village cricket match, the full essay has been reprinted plenty of times; here, if you can stomach them, are some of the worst excesses.

The elevens wore at their waists a rose, a red rose for the school girls, for the others a Maréchal Niel; and the victorious side were to leave the field with the rose of the vanquished at their belts.

The captains tossed for first innings in a professional manner: but, owing to a little peculiarity in one of them, who could not toss the coin without throwing up the other arm also, the penny was lost and a postage stamp had to be used; it answered all requirements and was slow in coming down, thus adding to the suspense. Then the Maréchal Niels went to the wickets, of course padless, carrying their bats beneath their arms, while the tail of the 'out' side gathered round the crease to hem in the ball and have a little chat until it came their way. The first representatives of the yellow rose were Miss Rawlins and Miss Thoms, who both played at least as well as a junior boys' team and with fairly straight bats, Miss Thoms getting the first cheer for going out and patting the ground with her bat. The attack was entrusted to Miss Mitchell (swift daisy-cutters) and a tall girl familiarly addressed as 'Georgie' (overhand). The first over was a maiden, but off Georgie's second ball Miss Rawlins scored 1; following it up shortly afterwards by lifting Miss Mitchell heftily to the on for 2. The running between wickets was much faster than that of boys, once the batswomen started, but they lost time in watching the flight of the ball. Miss Thoms gave point a chance off a hard one, which was not taken, and then skied Georgie straight above short mid-on, who shouted 'Mary dear.' I found that 'Mary dear,' at present cover point, was their great catcher, and that wherever the ball was lofted the fieldswomen usually shouted for her. . . .

The next comer was Miss Philips, who immediately opened out to a tempting one from Georgie, and put her away to leg for 3. For this only 2 should have been scored; but long leg, instead of returning the ball, ran smartly with it to the stumps and put it personally into the wicket-keeper's hands. . . .

Hilarious stuff, isn't it? Don't worry, it gets even worse.

Thirty was brought on soon afterwards in byes, no long-stop apparently being securable who would do more than hasten alongside the ball. . . .

Further disaster befell the 'in' side in the next over, Miss Thoms knocking off the bails with the skirt of her dress three times while turning to see whether Mary was fielding at long leg. She was then given out. Out she went in the jolliest way. They were all like that. Mary caught Miss Curson, and then the only altercation of the match arose, the Maréchal Niel captain coming out to complain that Mary was catching too many, and had no right to catch balls hit in the direction of another fielder.

After consultation between the umpires the decision was given in Mary's favour. . . .

The innings of the red rose was opened by Mary dear and Miss Wace, to the bowling of Mrs French and Miss Leslie. Mary took the first over from Miss Leslie, who has a dangerous delivery, pitching her balls so high that it is extremely difficult to reach them. Mary, however, has a leap that can reach anything, and 10 soon went up. The scoring now became fast and furious, Mary obtaining a complete mastery of the bowling and becoming so excited that she attempted once to catch herself.

In other words, even when one of the women in the match proves to be a good natural cricketer, Barrie can't restrain himself from making an unfair, snide crack at her expense.

With the score at 20, Mrs Tetch was tried at the pavilion end, but was only allowed to bowl one over, Mary hitting her so hard that it took five fielders to bring the ball back.

At 26 Miss Wace, whose shoe-lace had become undone, hit her wickets while retying it, and the next comer got a blob. . . . Mary continued to smite them; but was at last dismissed by a cup of cocoa brought to her amid applause, or at any rate by the next ball, which fell into the hands of Miss Leslie, who found it there after looking for it on the ground. After a short interval for what was evidently the most delightful conversation, play was resumed. . . . a remarkable change came over the aspect of the game when Miss Curson was put on to bowl. In her first over she almost did the hat trick, her delivery being so swift that even the slips fled. . . . At 42 Miss Croall would have been run out if Mrs Tetch had not paused to dust the ball before returning it. . . .

When all is said and done, however, the match was Mary dear's, who, I am incredibly informed, is a school-marm and the mother of two. I was also told that she cried on the way home because she thought she was such a rotten catcher. . . .

Now, if anyone had written such stuff – even as long ago as 1930 – about a cricket match between blacks, say, or

Jews, there would quite rightly have been an outcry, and the essay would have been omitted with distaste from all subsequent cricketing anthologies on the grounds that it was racist tosh. However, as I say, it has frequently been reprinted and, to judge from the general (but not quite universal) silence on the matter of its being rather in poor taste, one must assume that the various anthologists approve of it, and find the antics of those dear, delightful, delicate empty-headed dolls thigh-slappingly funny. The only possible riposte is ... but it had already been written, long before Barrie's time, by the Duke of Dorset in 1777 (and cited by Ford in his *Cricket: A Social History*):

Methinks I hear some little macaroni youth, some trifling apology for the figure of a man, exclaiming, with the greatest vehemence, How can the ladies hurt their delicate hands, and even bring them to blisters with holding a nasty, filthy bat? How can their sweet delicate fingers bear the jarrings attending the catching of a dirty ball? Are they not afraid lest the ball should displace an ivory tooth or extinguish the fire of an eye, which has long been considered a blazing meteor in the horizon of beauty, and which has brought many a roving, obdurate, and flinty heart to a true sense of its duty? Are not the soft charms of music, accompanied with the melody of the female voice, and the delight of their conversation, more irresistible than all the masculine sports they can usurp? And is there not reason to believe that, if cricket should become the favourite sport of their ladies, they will not learn fencing, and kill half of us in duels? Mind not, my dear ladies, the impertinent interrogatories of silly coxcombs, or the dreadful misapprehensions of demi-men. Let your sex go on and assert their right to every pursuit that does not debase the mind. Go on, and attach yourselves to the athletic; and by that convince your neighbours the French that you despise their washes, their paint, and their pomatums, and that you are determined to convince all Europe how worthy you are of being considered the wives of plain, generous and native Englishmen.

Hmmm. That more or less sums it up. Dorset was writing in the eighteenth century, of course, and so we may not agree with his every sentiment. But the next time you hear a bonehead sounding off about the evils of women mixing with cricket, look at him for what he really is, a 'little macaroni youth, some trifling apology for the figure of a man'. Even if he has all the brawn in the world, the description still stands. Some men are coxcombs in their heads.

On reflection, perhaps we could have done with a Betty Snowball, an Alison Uttley, a Rachael Heyhoe Flint, a Lucy Ridsdale, a Caroline Hill – or even, for that matter, my daughter – because we've just been rather comprehensively stuffed by the Quakkers. At least it hasn't been a total whitewash: a mere six wickets in it. I've taken two of the wickets to fall, and Jonty the other two. We're both feeling slightly pleased with ourselves (who ever said this was a team game?) because all the other bowlers have been hammered to far corners of the ground, and even beyond. In addition, I've taken the best caught-and-bowled of my life, which means that the feat was of about the same standard as you'll see several times an afternoon on the average cricket ground. Still . . .

Catherine and Jane have turned up, looking rather cold after their country ramble. The fog, which has considerably hovered overhead most of the afternoon, has now descended like a hawk on its prey or, more accurately, like that giant foot in *Monty Python's Flying Circus*. Darkness scurries over the pitch in pursuit, so that within a very few minutes of the game ending we are all blundering around half-blindly. Fortunately, the clubhouse bar has opened, and is sending out its bright yellow light over a reasonably sized arc of grass.

Davy, with the help of – I'm virtually certain – about a

litre of lighter fuel, has got the barbecue glowing, and the first chops are beginning to sizzle. We're working on the principle of pork chops, the largest you've ever seen, for the adults and burgers for the kids; I have a sly suspicion that this latter may be a mistake, because kids these days are getting sophisticated about the stuff they thrust down their throats. Jane, for example, has already collected herself a paper-plateful of mixed salad and is munching her way through it with enthusiasm if little elegance, and looks quite dismayed when her mother points out that she's got to eat a chop or a burger *as well*, because we've paid for it. I volunteer to help out by eating Jane's chop for her, but am silenced with a sparky glance.

And all too soon, of course, it's all over. The Quakkers and their friends wipe their lips and head for their cars amid cries of 'See you next year' and 'We must make this an annual event'. All of us mill around, helping with the clearing up – in fact, the job would be done a bit quicker if there were fewer helpers, but no one wants to look like a shirker. A party of kids are located, after a panicky torchlit search, on the far side of the ground, and are herded back to join the rest of us. Car doors slam – first of all only the odd one, then a more rapid succession. Sleepy kids scream. Davy gives me a cold pork chop, on the grounds that it's cooked already, and will only have to be thrown out if I don't eat it.

And then Catherine, Jane and I are walking down a pitch-black country lane, with high Devonian hedges on either side of us. Every now and then we have to dive into one of those hedges as a set of car-lights approaches – not easy for me, because I'm carrying a cake tin, with most of a Dundee cake in it and trying to eat a cold pork chop; and not easy for Catherine, because by now she's carrying Jane.

Home to the campsite, and the blare of all those

television sets. Trips to the latrines, and sneaky dis-
obedience of the NO SMOKING signs – until I spot the
mirrors in the ceiling. Blowing up the lilos. Bedding down
the brat. Speculating about why half the men going to the
Gents seem to be holding hands: perhaps the two main
meanings of the word 'camp' have converged? Falling
asleep, for Jane and Catherine; reading for a while for
me in flickering torchlight, because I've had enough
shandy to make it a good idea for me not to get undressed
for an hour or so.

The end of a season; my stomach's full of good food,
and I took that caught-and-bowled. Still, still, it's the end
of a season.

Part Three
1985

7
THE DREAM MATCH
16th March, 1985

'Only another couple of weeks 'til the first nets of the season,' I announce cheerfully to my wife, practising my bowling action, hammering my fist against the kitchen ceiling light, breezily swivelling around with the easy grace of a superbly trained athlete, and settling down in my chair to look gloomily at my breakfast plateful of wholemeal salt-free porridge. 'And it's going to be a really great season, I just *know* it,' I add with a fraction less conviction.

'That's what you always say in March, darling,' she says. 'Jane, take your elbow out of your muesli! Just wait until September, and tell me it all again.'

'But I know it's going to be really great,' I insist. 'I feel it in every sinew in my soul . . . or something. I can smell it in the air.'

'Oh, yeah.'

'I feel so bloody *fit* this Spring,' I say, removing my daughter's affectionate but jam-encrusted hand from my jersey, 'what with giving up booze, and cutting down on smoking, and eating all this – oh, God – healthy fat-free, salt-free, low-cholesterol . . . and *utterly delicious* food. Look,' I pat what's left of my paunch, 'I'm becoming like a lithe panther again, just like when we got married.'

'A lithe but pregnant panther,' she corrects.

'Are you going to be playing cricket on television, Daddy?' asks Jane.

'Perhaps not,' I concede.

'I'll believe you've had a really great season when you've had it,' says Catherine acidly, 'and not a moment before. By the way, don't forget that the zip on your whites has packed up.'

'I know it's going to be good,' I say, hugging my secret knowledge to myself for just one moment longer before saying: 'You see, I had this utterly amazing precognitive dream last night. I was . . . I was playing cricket, and I was bowling like a mad thing, and the stumps were flying everywhere, except the odd time when I took a caught-and-bowled, and then later on I was batting, and whatever I did the ball was going to the boundary, and . . .'

'And,' says my wife, 'how many runs did you score?' Her voice is oddly weary.

'I don't know,' I admit, 'but it must have been quite a lot. I *tell* you, it had all the hallmarks of a precognitive dream – I mean, I'm the expert on dreams in this family, so I should know.'

Catherine sits down, and with sadistic emphasis covers her own porridge with about a pint of milk and half a kilo of sugar. 'Sweetheart,' she says, like a teacher about to explain the facts of life to a class of rowdy eleven-year-olds, 'if I were you I wouldn't bother to 'phone the Society for Psychical Research until September.'

I take another mouthful of porridge, and the rest of breakfast-time passes in comparative silence.

APPENDIX

The Primary Club

All of us who play at the lowlier levels of cricket derive a great deal of pleasure from the sport; our club subscriptions, match fees and so on constitute excellent value in terms of the amount of pleasure gained for each penny invested. For an exceptionally small extra expense, virtually anyone at our level of cricket can have the additional advantage of knowing that their cricketing exploits can contribute to others who have more difficulty in getting something directly from the noblest game: the blind children of Dorton House, Sevenoaks, Kent. You – yes, *you* – can increase your enjoyment of the cricketing season, while contributing to a worthwhile cause, by joining the Primary Club.

This club was founded in 1955 by various members of the Beckenham Cricket Club who had displayed their considerable skills in losing their wicket to the first ball of any innings they 'played'. Apart from a modest subscription, they contributed a small 'fine' to the charity each time thereafter that they were out for a golden duck, and each time they were spotted by other members in failing to wear the club tie on specified occasions. Over the years, interest in the club's activities grew, so that now all of us are free to join: worldwide membership in 1984 was over 14,000, and the countries represented were Australia, Canada, Denmark, Greenland, Holland, Hong Kong, India, Iran, Iraq, Kenya, Malawi, Malaysia, Malta, New Zealand, Pakistan, South Africa, Uganda, the United Kingdom, the United States of America, the West Indies, and Zimbabwe. The sums raised for charity, after minimal deductions for the manufacture of ties, postage, etc., were £12,000 in 1981, £14,000 in 1982, £16,000 in 1983 and £18,000 in 1984.

Dorton House School for Blind Children has benefited considerably from these donations. The club's honorary secretary, Leslie Harris, was able to report in his April 1984 newsletter to members that the Primary Club had paid in full for a £50,000 new gymnasium and a £10,000 minibus for the school; in April 1985 he recorded that the club had raised enough money for a ski-slope for the use of the children, and was now setting aside money for the construction of an adventure playground and the purchase of some ponies. If you have sighted children of your own, you will know how much we all take for granted the fact that they can have access at school or elsewhere to sporting facilities such as gymnasia; blind children, whose need for such things is even greater, have to rely on the generosity of people like the members of the Primary Club in order to enjoy what are, in terms of their personal development as individuals, virtually necessities.

Should you wish to join the Primary Club, be assured that the donations required from you are unlikely to strain your finances; if you can afford a couple of pints after a game, then you're not going to miss the modest sums involved in joining the club. As of the year 1985, the minimum investment involved was an initial fee of £3·50 (for which you received a club tie) plus an annual subscription of at least 50p. Each time a member was out first ball, he or she had to send at least 12½p to the club. A member failing to wear the tie on the first Saturday of each month during the season, on the Saturday of any Lord's Test, or at a Primary Club function, and spotted so doing by any other member of the club was obliged to donate a further 12½p as well as buy the eagle-eyed 'friend' a drink.

For slightly higher initial fees, new members can receive different ties – a 'City' model in navy blue rather than the green of the standard version, or a broader tie in the 'City' colours. Alternatively, you can pay an initial fee of £10·00, which not only gives you life membership of the club but entitles you to both the standard and the 'City' ties – a very good deal indeed. The ties are extremely attractive, and you could easily spend more than ten pounds buying two ties of similar quality in the shops.

How can you go about joining? Well, first of all you have to be out to the first ball you face in a match. In theory, you should be able, when applying, to specify the date and other details of this event, but in practice the club is prepared to take your word for it: you probably wouldn't be reading this book if you hadn't qualified several times over. If you're one of those rare birds who has *never* recorded a golden duck (and I'm not sure I believe you), then don't worry about it: you can apply for special dispensation from the committee to allow you to join anyway. Female cricketers are as eligible as male ones, and members' spouses can join, too, if they wish; female spouses and cricketers are expected to wear a club brooch rather than necessarily a club tie on the occasions noted above.

For a copy of the rules, a recent report on fund-raising activities and an application form, write to L. J. Harris, Honorary Secretary, The Primary Club, 14 Shrewsbury Road, Beckenham, Kent (tel.: 01-650 0936) or, if you are reading this book many years after its first publication and since Mr Harris must retire someday, c/o Beckenham Cricket Club, Foxgrove Road, Beckenham, Kent. Although Leslie Harris does not insist upon it, obviously it would be sensible for you to enclose a stamped, self-addressed envelope or, if you live outside the UK, an international reply coupon or sufficient cash to cover the return postage; if you don't do this then it is the children of Dorton House who will be paying for your failure.

So go on: write today.

ACKNOWLEDGEMENTS

Many people have helped me in my quest for tales of cricketing at its finest: some have written to me – often at great length – while others have bent my ear in pubs and then later been good enough to remind me of the data buried in my pickled braincells.

In no particular order, the main correspondents have been
- Bill Pullen, of Gotherington CC.
- Colin Cracknell, of Heston CC.
- Ronnie Locke, of Cheadle Hulme CC.
- Paul Sylvester, late of Hendon School.
- John Trevisick, who went far beyond the call of duty in giving me the stark truth about clerical cricket.

The primary conversationalists have been
- Malcolm Couch, of the West Country Publishers' CC.
- Vic Giolitto, of the West Country Publishers' CC.
- John Pierce, recently of Devonair and occasionally of the West Country Publishers' CC.
- Simon Strong, of the *Western Morning News* CC.
- Geoffrey Household, of the West Country Publishers' CC.
- Bill Bailey, of the West Country Publishers' CC and the Maggie is Magic Brigade.
- Adrian Male, of Whimple CC.
- Dave Parsons, cricketing mercenary extraordinary.

Others of note are

● Rt Hon. Roy Hattersley MP, who gave me permission to pillage his various published cricketing memories.

● Professor Sir Bernard Lovell, who gave similar permission in connection with his essay 'The Moon Match'.

● L. J. Carter, Executive Secretary of the British Interplanetary Society, who gave me advice about astronomers (aside from the standard 'count the forks').

● Michael Mates MP, who allowed me access to information about Lords & Commons Cricket; Susan Carter, his secretary, who found the time to talk with me at length about our politicians' cricketing activities; and Corinne Bell, his research assistant, although 'all I did was make a xerox for you' (true, but it was the timing of the xerox that mattered).

● Keith Harper, who wrote to me about the annual Press versus TUC matches.

● David Langford, who published an unsuccessful appeal in *Ansible*.

● Hal Robinson, who lent me *In Praise of Cricket* and never ticked me off for holding onto it far longer than I'd promised.

● Phil Gardner of Asgard, who gave me *The World's Best Cricket Book Ever*.

● Keith Barnett, who gave me *The Penguin Cricketer's Companion* for my birthday.

● Neil Gaiman, who arranged that I be sent a review copy of *Ghastly Beyond Belief* and so introduced me to the magic of Victor Wadey.

● Nick Austin of Granada Publishing, who has somehow managed to retain faith in this book ever since it was no more than a glint in my eye, and whose support has been invaluable – perhaps 'encouragement' would be a better word.

● Catherine and Jane Barnett, for reasons outwith the scope of this book.

A number of people have very kindly given me their free permission (often in very friendly tones) to quote their copyright work: these are William Trevor, George Mikes, Alan Rusbridger and Allen Synge. My very sincere thanks to them. Others who have granted me permission to quote copyright material and to whom I am grateful are:

● The Estate of J. M. Barrie (extracts from *The Greenwood Hat*; with special thanks to Amanda Smith for her sterling work in sorting out the whole business for me)
● John Murray Ltd. (extract from *A Pattern of Islands* by Arthur Grimble)
● Faber & Faber Ltd. (extract from *Carts and Candlesticks* by Alison Uttley)
● Century Hutchinson Ltd. (extract from *Beyond a Boundary* by C. L. R. James)
● Hodder & Stoughton Ltd. (extract from *The Best Loved Game* by Geoffrey Moorhouse)

The extract from Robert Graves' *Goodbye to All That* is reproduced by permission of A. P. Watt Ltd.

Pan Books Ltd granted permission to quote the extract from *Life, The Universe and Everything* by Douglas Adams.

I've used my every best endeavour to contact the owners of copyright material quoted in this book. If, nevertheless, you feel that I've used somthing of yours without the due permission, please accept my apologies and write to me care of the publishers.

BIBLIOGRAPHY

As in earlier books of mine, I have denoted by * works whose indexes are inadequate and by ** the depressingly many works which have been published without an index at all. Editions cited are those which I've consulted, and need not necessarily be the earliest.

** Arlott, John (ed.): *My Favourite Cricket Stories*, Guildford and London, Lutterworth, 1974.

** Aye, John (ed.): *In Praise of Cricket*, London, Muller, 1946.

** Barrie, J. M.: *The Greenwood Hat*, London, Peter Davies, 1937.

Birkin, Andrew: *J. M. Barrie and the Lost Boys*, London, Constable, 1979.

** Boddey, Martin (ed.): *The Twelfth Man: A Book of Original Contributions Brought Together by the Lord's Taverners*, London, Cassell, 1971.

** Brayshaw, Ian: *The Wit of Cricket*, London, Deutsch, 1982.

** Bullus, Eric E.: *A History of Lords and Commons Cricket*, London, Blades, East and Blades, n.d. but c1958.

**Dickens, Charles: 'Sunday Under Three Heads', 1836, in *The Uncommercial Traveller and Reprinted Pieces, etc.*, London, Oxford University Press, 1958.

Dupré, Catherine: *John Galsworthy: A Biography*, London, Collins, 1976.

* Edwards, Owen Dudley: *The Quest for Sherlock Holmes*, Harmondsworth, Penguin, 1984.

** Elwin, Malcolm (ed.): *Devon Dumplings Cricket Club Jubilee Book 1902–1952*, South Devon, privately published, n.d. but *c*1953.

Flint, Rachael Heyhoe, and Rheinberg, Netta: *Fair Play: The Story of Women's Cricket*, London, Angus and Robertson, 1976.

** Fogg, John: *The Haig Book of Village Cricket*, London, Pelham, 1972.

Ford, John: *Cricket: A Social History 1700–1835*, Newton Abbot, David and Charles, 1972.

Frindall, Bill: *The Guinness Book of Cricket Facts and Feats*, Enfield, Guinness Superlatives, 1983.

** Gaiman, Neil, and Newman, Kim: *Ghastly Beyond Belief*, London, Arrow, 1985.

* Grant, John: *A Book of Numbers*, Bath, Ashgrove Press, 1982.

** Green, Benny (ed.): *The Cricket Addict's Archive*, London, Elm Tree, 1977.

** Hattersley, Roy: *Politics Apart: A Selection of* Listener *Endpieces*, London, BBC, 1982.

** Hattersley, Roy: *A Yorkshire Boyhood*, London, Chatto and Windus, 1983.

Higham, Charles: *The Adventures of Conan Doyle*, London, Hamish Hamilton, 1976.

** Holles, Robert: *The Guide to Real Village Cricket*, London, Harrap, 1983.

* Howatt, Gerald: *Village Cricket*, Newton Abbot, David and Charles, 1980.

James, C. L. R.: *Beyond a Boundary*, London, Stanley Paul, 1963.

* Kilburn, J. M.: *Overthrows: A Book of Cricket*, London, Stanley Paul, 1975.

* Marrot, H. V.: *The Life and Letters of John Galsworthy*, London, Heinemann, 1935.

** Mell, George: *This Curious Game of Cricket*, London, George Allen and Unwin, 1982.

** Moorhouse, Geoffrey: *The Best Loved Game*, London, Hodder and Stoughton, 1979.

Ormerod, G. Wareing: *Annals of the Teignbridge Cricket Club 1823–1883*, Teignmouth, privately published, 1888.

** Parkinson, Michael: *Cricket Mad*, London, Stanley Paul, 1969.

** Raven, Simon: *Shadows on the Grass*, London, Blond and Briggs, 1982.

* Ross, Alan (ed.): *The Penguin Cricketer's Companion* (revised edn of *The Cricketer's Companion*, 1960), Harmondsworth, Penguin, 1981.

** Sherwood, Peter, and Alderdice, Gary: *The World's Best Cricket Book Ever*, East Ardsley, EP, n.d. but *c*1982.

** Simons, Eric N.: *Friendly Eleven*, London, Werner Laurie, 1950.

** Synge, Allen (ed.): *Strangers' Gallery*, London, Lemon Tree Press, 1974.

** Tarrant, Graham: *The Lord's Taverners Cricket Quiz Book*, Newton Abbot, David and Charles, 1984.

Thorpe, James: *Happy Days*, London, Gerald Howe, 1933.

** Wells, H. G.: *Certain Personal Matters*, London, Lawrence and Bullen, 1898.

Index

INDEX

A selection of humour titles available in Panther Books

Michael Bentine
The Best of Bentine £1.95 ☐

Lenny Bruce
How to Talk Dirty and Influence People £1.95 ☐

Rae Andre and Peter Ward
The 59-Second Employee £1.95 ☐

Dai Lintone
Good Connections £1.95 ☐

Arthur Marshall
I'll Let You Know £1.95 ☐
Smile, Please £1.95 ☐

P J O'Rourke
Modern Manners £2.50 ☐

Harry Chance
The Bounder's Companion £1.95 ☐

Simon Langford
The Left-Handed Book £1.95 ☐

Dr Barbara Lovehouse
No Bad Men: Training Men the Lovehouse Way £1.50 ☐

To order direct from the publisher just tick the titles you want
and fill in the order form. **GF2481**

The best in biography from Panther Books

John Brooke
King George III   £1.95 ☐

J Bryan III and Charles J V Murphy
The Windsor Story   £2.95 ☐

Margaret Forster
The Rash Adventurer   £1.25 ☐

Antonia Fraser
Mary Queen of Scots   £3.95 ☐
Cromwell: Our Chief of Men   £3.95 ☐

Eric Linklater
The Prince in the Heather   £2.50 ☐

Henri Troyat
Catherine the Great   £2.95 ☐

Sir Arthur Bryant
Samuel Pepys: The Man in the Making   £3.95 ☐
Samuel Pepys: The Years of Peril   £3.95 ☐

To order direct from the publisher just tick the titles you want
and fill in the order form.   **GB181**

Books of historical interest now available in Panther Books

David Daiches
Edinburgh (illustrated)   £1.95 ☐
Glasgow (illustrated)   £2.50 ☐

Paul Johnson
The National Trust Book of British Castles (illustrated)   £3.95 ☐

Nigel Nicolson
The National Trust Book of Great Houses (illustrated)   £3.95 ☐

Frank Delaney
James Joyce's Odyssey (illustrated)   £2.95 ☐

Stan Gébler Davies
James Joyce: A Portrait of the Artist   £1.95p ☐

Peter Somerville-Large
Dublin (illustrated)   £2.25 ☐

To order direct from the publisher just tick the titles you want
and fill in the order form.   **GM681**

The best in biography from Panther Books

Lee McCann
Nostradamus: The Man Who Saw Through Time   £2.50   ☐

Larry Collins & Dominique Lapierre
Or I'll Dress You in Mourning   £1.25   ☐

Ladislas Farago
Patton: Ordeal and Triumph   £1.50   ☐

Hermann Hesse
A Pictorial Biography   £1.50   ☐

A E Hotchner
Papa Hemingway   £1.25   ☐

Nell Kimball
My Life as an American Madam   £1.50   ☐

Doris Lessing
In Pursuit of the English   £1.50   ☐

Stan Gébler Davies
James Joyce – A Portrait of the Artist   £1.95   ☐

Jean Stein & George Plimpton
Edie: An American Biography   £3.95   ☐

To order direct from the publisher just tick the titles you want
and fill in the order form.   **GB281**

Regional books in Panther Books

Showell Styles
Welsh Walks and Legends   £1.00 ☐

Chris Barber
Mysterious Wales   £2.50 ☐

Brian J. Bailey
Lakeland Walks and Legends   £1.50 ☐

Robert Orrell
Saddle Tramp in the Lake District   £1.50 ☐

Tom Weir
Weir's Way   £2.50 ☐

David Daiches
Edinburgh   £1.95 ☐
Glasgow   £2.50 ☐

Peter Somerville-Large
Dublin   £2.25 ☐

Frank Delaney
James Joyce's Odyssey   £2.95 ☐

Mary Cathcart Borer
London Walks and Legends   £1.95 ☐

Mary Peplow & Debra Shipley
London for Free   £1.95 ☐

To order direct from the publisher just tick the titles you want
and fill in the order form.   HB1281

All these books are available at your local bookshop or newsagent, or can be ordered direct from the publisher.

To order direct from the publisher just tick the titles you want and fill in the form below.

Name _____

Address _____

_____

Send to:
Panther Cash Sales
PO Box 11, Falmouth, Cornwall TR10 9EN.

Please enclose remittance to the value of the cover price plus:

UK 45p for the first book, 20p for the second book plus 14p per copy for each additional book ordered to a maximum charge of £1.63.

BFPO and Eire 45p for the first book, 20p for the second book plus 14p per copy for the next 7 books, thereafter 8p per book.

Overseas 75p for the first book and 21p for each additional book.